An Observer's Guide

Materials & Techniques of Collage

Home and Garden

The Herb Grower's Guide
Car Care

Art and Craft

Pencil Drawing
Drawing with Ink
Using Pastels
Beginning Watercolour
Materials and Techniques of Oil Painting
Materials and Techniques of Watercolour
Materials and Techniques of Acrylic Painting
Materials and Techniques of Collage
Let's Make Pottery
First Steps in Upholstery

Where Is It?

Paintings and Sculpture of the Fifteenth Century
Italian, French and Spanish Paintings of the Seventeenth Century
Dutch and Flemish Paintings of the Seventeenth Century
British Paintings—Hogarth to Turner
European Paintings of the Eighteenth Century
British Paintings of the Nineteenth Century
European Paintings of the Nineteenth Century
Twentieth Century Paintings—Bonnard to Rothko

AN OBSERVER'S GUIDE

Materials & Techniques of Collage

John FitzMaurice Mills

FREDERICK WARNE

Published by Frederick Warne (Publishers) Ltd, London, 1981

ISBN 0 7232 2478 1

Printed and bound in Great Britain by
William Clowes (Beccles) Limited, Beccles and London
1499.1180

Contents

Foreword

Making pictures, whether abstract or realist, seems to fulfil some appetite for expression inside most of us. Numbers of would-be followers of this art may get discouraged by the methods and ways of the traditional techniques; they get that moment of fear, which has incidentally been shared by many a master artist, when the approach is made to the untouched piece of paper or canvas.

Collage is different with its demands. It is asking one to enjoy the experience of becoming involved with all manner of exciting and often strange materials, to evaluate these for their colour, their feel and texture and to join in a picture-creating experience that can be both a serious art form and a joyful and imaginative method of visual expression possible for anyone.

The initial cost for the first experiments need be little more than the price of a tube of glue. The reward can be a release of ideas. A period with bits and pieces of waste things, brushes, paints, scissors, pins, paste and the rest can result in surprisingly satisfying moments.

History and development

The name appears to have been evolved from the French term *papier collé*, which roughly translated implies the sticking of certain materials together, to form a pictorial composition. Probably the earliest known examples occurred in the late 18th century with the making of simple pictures by sticking dried ferns on to cards and paper. In the following century it became a popular pastime to prepare birthday and greeting cards in this way, a variety of materials being used; for example sea shells, dried flowers, ribbons, cut-out paper forms and other fragments that took the eye of the maker. The nearest these collages would have come to being called an art form was with the skilfully cut silhouettes, generally black images on a white ground, but sometimes white images on a black ground. The latter were not always true silhouettes as features and small details were added.

But come the beginning of this century, when many artists were experimenting widely with techniques, collage suddenly grew up and became a recognized method of picture-making for the professional. It is

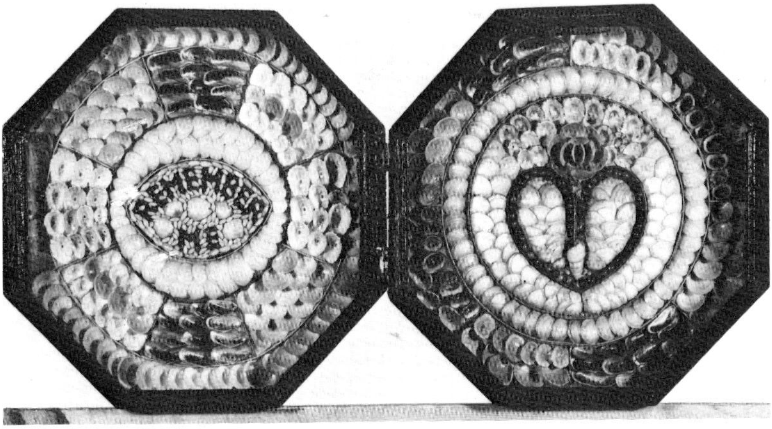

Nineteenth-century valentine in a glazed case, worked with shells and grains of corn *(Courtesy of Christie's, South Kensington)*

recorded that in 1908 Pablo Picasso pasted a small piece of paper on the centre of *La Rève*, a drawing he was working on, and by repute had made the first fine-art *papier collé* or collage. From this he progressed three years later to what might be termed a fully integrated collage with *Still Life with Chair Caning*. In this he used a piece of ordinary oilcloth with a design that showed the caning as found in a seat of a chair, and over it he painted a series of bold abstract and near abstract forms. The whole was carried out on an oval support—a fashion being experimented with by the Cubists as a revolt against the rectangle, which had dominated painting shapes since the Renaissance.

Others were soon to join the exploration of this exciting method for visual expression. Within about 12 months Georges Braque was producing such as *Le Courrier*, basically a linear pattern with added wallpapers or newsprint. At the end of the First World War the German George Grosz saw collage as a way to heighten some of his savage social satires. In *Germany, a Winter's Tale* he reduced the background to a broken kaleidoscope of Berlin, and on to this he superimposed scraps of newsprint and large painted figures. Others who were to try this method of picture-making included Max Ernst, Henri Matisse, Kurt Schwitters and the American Robert Motherwell.

It was Max Ernst who was to give one of the earliest lucid explanations as to just how these experimenters worked.

> . . . we would come by chance, or as it seemed by chance, on (for example) the pages of a catalogue containing plates for anatomical or physical demonstration and found that these provided contiguously figurative elements so mutually distant that the very absurdity of their collection produced in us a hallucinating succession of contradictory images, superimposed one upon another with the persistence and rapidity proper to amorous recollections. These images themselves brought forth a new plane in order to meet in a new unknown (the plane of non-suitability).

Ernst and others with a surrealist approach saw collage as a way to express the fantasies they felt in their subconscious without having to be too deeply involved with the strictures of established techniques, as imposed by the traditional methods of painting. Here they were developing something that could employ all the techniques from the past that they might choose to use plus all kinds of ideas that were rapidly being invented. Briefly, this collage that was emerging was what the French might term an *assemblage* of an astonishing array of contrasting materials. Today the method has evolved into a process in which almost 'anything goes'.

Approaching collage for the first time can be a bewildering experience if more normal and staid techniques are held in mind. The more successful works produced have in general been those that are free in their conception and execution. Try not to get caught up with a too-natural imagery. This visual creative experience is something that is concerned with not only colour and form but also texture and off-beat relationships, as pointed to by Ernst. In some ways it is a more total absorption for the artist than is a traditional method. The imagination can come into contact with enlivening visual material and can direct the hands in the early stages of arrangement before the composition is fixed. It is perhaps this point of free arrangement that holds much of the attraction and educative value of collage.

First there is the training of the eye to find those materials that can contrast with each other. Then, having surrounded oneself with the heterogeneous array, begin the building up of the idea; or perhaps even wait to see an idea develop as the materials are brought against one another. In a matter of not many minutes half a dozen rough thoughts can be run through, tried out, followed up or discarded.

This visual manipulation can prove extremely stimulating. One new contrast can trigger off a whole series of hitherto untried or undared uses for form, colour and texture. These preliminary steps will not only make for more satisfying work later with collage but will also be of considerable help with painting. These arrangements and formations can serve to give courage, particularly to the beginner.

For those who have not tried the technique of collage, it can open up a diversity that can prove exciting and satisfying. The experience is really open to all. There is little economic restriction, as a large part of the materials come under the heading of waste. Tools required are few and basic. Elaborate studios are not called for; most can work happily on the kitchen table.

As the early steps are taken, what points are helpful to watch for? First that this idea of artistic freedom is truly grasped and that you do not let in some restricting convention from the past. Academic rulings might say that some ideas are not compatible. Don't be put off, go right ahead and try them out. Collage can be a very personal method of expression, and you may find that you come across a particular manner that will be your individual way. Secondly, if you are in the habit of keeping sketchbooks or roughing out ideas on paper, never throw them away. They can be material from which some later theme may grow or be incorporated in differing ways in a composition. Artists such as Jean Dubuffet and Willem De Kooning have worked forms and figures that started as quick sketches into compositions, often giving them fresh vitality by placing them at varying angles to the original intention or throwing them into contrast by the use of colours and unexpected textures. Thirdly, be on the look-out for new things; keep a notebook for comments on the unusual, materials seen, odd techniques that have been tried out by others.

Collage in the widest sense is the organization of materials and ways to use them. It can be restricted to the simplest of torn paper work, or progress through to an elaborate handling of textiles, cards, pieces of wood, powders, gravel, bones and metal scrap. It can be half painting and half stuck-on material. The painting can underly the applied substances or it may be over them. The intricacies of photomontage can be explored. Old coloured magazine advertisements can be a rich source from which to build up forceful imagery that can be often hilarious, dramatic and serious or abstract.

Tools

Brushes

The number of these and the different types chosen will depend on the methods of collage that are to be worked on.

One basic brush should be a fairly good quality household decorator's with a width of between 25 and 40 mm (1–1½ in). This can be used in a number of ways; namely, sizing and priming the supports, laying down materials with adhesives, painting broad areas, applying consolidating liquids to frail materials and for spatter work.

A round wire-bound glue brush is helpful if working with the glues applied hot, such as hoof or rabbit-skin. This can also be used with cold-water pastes.

Round and flat hog-bristle brushes of about No. 6 size and also No. 5 round and No. 7 flat oxhair brushes will serve as a beginner's set for painting with oils, acrylics, tempera, gouache or watercolour.

A point to watch with the care of the brushes is that they are cleaned with the right liquids. In collage work the brushes are often given a fair knocking about, and also they will be used with a number of different materials that will only dissolve with certain solvents. After use with oil paints the brushes should be well rinsed out with white spirit. If used with acrylics, generally they will clean out with copious rinsing in clean water, but if the colour has hardened they will have to be left soaking in alcohol or methylated spirit for several hours. After working with tempera, gouache or watercolour, a good rinsing in water should clear the bristles or hairs. If a brush has been used with one or other of the synthetic glues, it will depend to a degree on the instructions for cleaning-up on the tube or container. Should none be given and a brush has hardened out, a short soaking in acetone will generally bring it clean. If this solvent is used, it is emphasized that there should be adequate ventilation and also precautions against fire. Brushes that have been employed with animal or fish glues, starch or flour paste will need little more than a rinsing in lukewarm water. To be quite sure the brush heads are as clean as possible, after the preliminary treatment they should all be washed out in lukewarm water with a little good quality plain soap, rinsed in plain water and then carefully moulded with the fingertips to their correct shapes. It is unwise to use detergents for cleaning brushes because some can damage the setting of the bristles or hairs.

Brushes, even of the lesser varieties, are now no longer cheap items and it is well worth looking after them. If they are to be stored away, place in their vicinity some material that will discourage clothes moths as these are partial to laying eggs in the hairs or bristles and the hatched-out larvae can wreck a brush head in a very short time. The best position in which to leave the brushes when they are not being used is upright in an old jar or similar container; or if placed in a drawer, build in a small ramp at an angle of around 15 degrees and lay them on this head up.

Clamps

Again, whether or not these are necessary will depend on the type of work planned. But certainly if low relief is envisaged using small slats of wood or pieces of metal sheet, two or three screw 'G' clamps will be of service. They should be as round in shape as possible to give them a good reach over the support. Their use will greatly facilitate the gluing down of the pieces, and make unnecessary the tedium of holding or the use of weights. Be careful not to damage the surface of the materials if a fair pressure has to be applied. It is a good idea to have one or two small pieces of scrap that can be placed between the jaws of the clamps and the materials being fixed.

Clips

Make a collection in a small box of a variety of wire clips of varying sizes, also some of those big metal paper clips with the jaws held by a round spring—plastic versions of the same type can be included. These will be of service for holding light materials when being glued and for holding different pieces in place during mock-up stages.

Files

It can be helpful to have one or two files of different sections, as they will come in handy for the treatment of metal edges, wood pieces, soft stones and other substances that call for a trim-up or slight alteration of shape.

Glue-pot

If much work is to be done with animal or fish glues, it is worth investing in a proper pot. This should be of heavy iron and consist of an outer container to hold the water and an inner for the glue. The latter fits quite snugly into the top of the outer to prevent too much heat loss when the water boils and also to cut down the escape of steam. A substitute if working with small amounts can be to use a small tin inside a slightly larger one. The pot can be heated on any convenient appliance, such as an electric ring, a gas ring, a primus or a slab range. If working in very cold weather, heat up gently as too sudden a fierce temperature could cause the toughest iron to crack.

Hammer

This need not be very heavy, as generally it will only be used with quite small nails or panel pins. Often a hammer comes with a handle that is too long for control and comfort. Depending on your hand size, it is more suitable to shorten the handle down to about 25 cm (10 in).

Knives

The craft knife that will take different-shaped blades is reliable and it will be able to tackle not only thick papers and cardboards but also thin wood slats. Keep old kitchen knives which, if of good quality plain steel, will take a sharp edge on a stone; and have handy a good penknife. If any of these get coated with synthetic glues, it is best to clean them as soon as possible before they set rock hard. Acetone (see the warning above under brushes) will clear even quite large lumps; otherwise these can sometimes be scraped loose with another knife. If doing this, make sure that there is a firm support under the blade to prevent warping.

Long or rat-nosed pliers

Choose a stout and reasonably large pair of these because they will be called upon to deal with not only cutting varying thicknesses of wire but also bending metal sheets and inserting and extracting nails and pins. Watch, when making the purchase, that the handles do not come together in a way that can give your fingers a vicious nip.

Painting knives

These are a little bit of a luxury, but they can be very useful for applying thick adhesives, pastes, plasters and colours. They can be made of steel or plastic; the former is the better by far for serious work. When making the selection, choose those with springy and pliant blades and with the handles cranked up so that the knuckles of the holding hand will be clear of the surface being worked on.

Pin pusher

This rather odd implement enables one to push steel dressmaking pins through heavy cardboards or straight into thick pulp boards without bending the slender shafts. It can also be used with thin panel pins if the heads are not too large. The mystery is explained by the fact that the pin is placed in the hollow tube at the end and when pressure is applied a small piston descends and drives it home.

Roller or brayer

This should be rubber or composition covered and around 100 to 120 mm (4 to 5 in) wide. It is excellent for smoothing down areas of laid papers or textiles and for spreading colour over wide surfaces.

Scalpels

Those used by surgeons are the best. The handles come in several sizes and there are a number of different blade shapes to choose from. If you have not used these before, watch out, for the blades really are sharp—so much so that it is quite possible to inflict a deep cut almost without feeling it. If they are left lying around and not being used, a safety measure can be to stick the tips of the blades into pieces of cork.

Scissors

For serious work, two pairs should be included. One exclusively for paper and thin card work and the other for textiles only; if the latter is used for paper as well this will tend to dull the cutting edges and then a clean cut will be impossible, and threads can be drawn.

If specialized work with fine detail is intended, it is worth including a small pair of embroidery scissors with fine pointed blades. For extensive work with fabrics, a pair of pinking shears that have saw teeth or serrated blades are also a useful addition. These will allow for the cutting of fabrics so that edges do not need a hem.

Scrapers

These items can be made easily. Scraps of metal sheet can be trimmed with the shears, small slats of wood shaped up with a knife, or heavy card cut out with a sharp blade. The working edges can be left straight or notched with comb-like teeth. The purpose for scrapers can vary from laying down wet plasters to the creating of textured paint surfaces; the metal ones can also be used for smoothing down rough areas on dried plaster or giving an adze-like finish to soft woods.

Screwdriver

Pick one with a handle that is comfortable to hold, and preferably with a ratchet because this greatly helps control and prevents slipping if working in an area close to upstanding materials.

Sharpening stone

This is worth having around so that knife blades are workmanlike. A sharp blade is often the safest to use, as it will cut properly without too much pressure which might cause a slip. There are two principal types: those that are worked with oils and those with water. When sharpening, try to hold the blade at the angle to which it was originally set; this will generally be about 20 degrees from the flat.

Small metal shears

Select a pair with a bite of at least 50 mm (2 in) and watch, as with the long-nosed pliers, that the handles are not likely to savage the fingers when in use.

Staple gun

This may be a luxury, but the extra expense will soon show its worth. It will enable metal staples to be driven cleanly into heavy cardboards, hardboards, chipboards, pulpboards and wood with accuracy and certainty.

Tweezers

If fine work is being attempted with small particles such as seeds, small shells or tiny metal fragments, a pair will be a blessing.

Materials for fixing

Acrylic paints

These may seem somewhat out of place under this heading. But it should be understood that the pigments are bound with a PVA emulsion and this will allow papers, textiles and many other dry materials to be stuck straight into the applied colours; the only proviso being that the paints intended for use in this manner should for the best results be put on thick and short as they come from the tubes. There is often some confusion over acrylic paints because they can be sometimes displayed under this name or polymer, PVA or other trade titles. The acrylic medium supplied for use with the paints can also be used as an adhesive and it should be handled in the same way as recommended for the paints.

Fixatives

These will not be used in the way that is employed to hold firm charcoal or pastel drawings; they will help to consolidate frail materials such as lace, wool or tissue papers. Normally the simplest way to apply them is after the materials have been glued into position; then the fixative can be gently sprayed over the chosen areas. One of the best substances for this is an acrylic medium that has been diluted with about two parts water to one of acrylic. Applications should be short and repeated as the previous coats dry. This will avoid the materials becoming soaked which could cause them to change appearance and also position. Diluted starch and weak size can be used in the same way. It can also be helpful to stiffen the backs of some fabrics with any of the above before they are fixed in position. Be careful not to drench the material, for if the fixative soaks through to the front it can cause discoloration.

Nails, panel pins and screws

Length and size of all these will depend on the materials being used. They are best kept in airtight containers to protect them from rust. If the heads are being painted over with a water-based glue or paint they should be sealed first with shellac dissolved to saturation point in methylated spirit or with a synthetic glue.

Natural glues

The principal natural glues are made of fish, hoof, horn and rabbit-skin. All these, being water soluble, should be used with a glue-pot. If instructions are on the packets, follow these carefully to attain the best mixture possible. The glue when ready should have the consistency of single cream and should be free of lumps. For a thinner adhesive or a size, more water can be added. Watch that the water in the outer container of the glue-pot does not boil dry and also never attempt to heat one of these glues in a single container directly over a heat source. If this is done, it will quite easily scorch and one of a fish variety can cause a truly dreadful smell.

Starch and flour paste can be useful, and both are simply prepared. Neither should be looked on as a truly permanent adhesive but they will serve for experimental work and also as stiffeners for some materials.

One other that can be mentioned here, although it is not a truly natural substance, is latex, which is made usable by the addition of a petroleum liquid. It is highly inflammable but has its uses, particularly when working out rough ideas, as it allows for very quick application by brush, painting knife or scraper. It can be a clean gum to use because any excess that goes over an area not intended can generally be rolled or pulled away with a fingertip or a piece of art gum cleaner.

Pins

A small tin of varied length pins should be at hand. The pins bought should be the normal dressmaking quality; the extra thin variety are not suitable as they bend very easily.

Staples

When possible it is best to procure the copper coated type as these will be resistant to rust.

Synthetic adhesives

There is a wide variety of these on the market and they come mainly under three headings: contact, epoxy and polyvinyl acetate (PVA).

The contact adhesives are nearly all water clear and a thin coating should be applied to both surfaces and left for about five minutes or until they are tacky. The glued surfaces should then be brought together and held firmly for the time specified on the containers or clamped or weighted and left for several hours or overnight. This group includes the so-called 'instant' glues that are virtually that. The adhesion time can be measured in seconds, so it is important that the components are brought together in the right place the first time. Read the notes carefully on the tubes before using, especially those referring to spillage on the fingers; generally hot water is advocated for removal. Try to avoid this happening as the glue will really stick skin to skin with remarkable strength.

Epoxy resin adhesives normally come in two tubes or tins, containing a base and a hardener. They should be mixed up just before use being sure that the two substances are thoroughly dispersed. Mixing is best done on a scrap piece of metal, an old saucer or a small pane of glass, using a steel knife to do the stirring and probably the applying. The setting times for these epoxy resins will vary between makes; the fastest averaging between five and ten minutes, others taking as long as 12 hours and even up to 24. As with the contacts, both surfaces should receive a thin coating and then be left to get tacky. After being brought together, the joins may be clamped, weighted or bound with self-adhesive tape.

In the main, when using the contact or epoxy, it is important that the areas to be joined should be scrupulously clean and thoroughly degreased. This can be done by wiping over with a swab of cotton wool dipped in methylated spirit and then allowing the surfaces to dry. It sometimes helps with the epoxy resins if the surfaces being joined are given a very slight tooth by being rubbed with a piece of fine sandpaper. It should be remembered that the contacts and epoxy resins can be toxic and should always be used where there is adequate ventilation; if any traces get on to the skin, the hands should be washed as soon as possible with warm soapy water.

The PVA adhesives come in tubes, plastic containers and jars and will appear as light milky liquids with a creamy consistency. Generally they should all dry out with a glass-like clearness, so do not be put off by this characteristic. As they are emulsions, they can be safely diluted with water; the amount of water will depend on the job in hand. For laying tissues, the mix can be as thin as one part PVA to five parts water; for normal paperwork one part PVA to three parts water; for textiles it is probably best to use it neat. But these suggested dilutions and treatment will depend very much on the materials being used, so that personal experiment is called for. The PVAs may also be mixed with substances such as sawdust, sands, kaolin, whiting, marble dust and other such to form pastes suitable for modelling or raising surfaces. When doing this, break down the PVAs to a ratio of about one part to three of water.

Apart from the foregoing, there are a number of adhesives and gums with widely varying trade names and descriptive uses, and more and more are being introduced onto the market. It is sometimes difficult to see in which group they fall. Try following the directions given, and experiment.

In general, failures with synthetic adhesives are caused by one or more of these reasons: surfaces being joined wet or greasy; one or other surface being unsympathetic to the adhesive (suitable materials to be joined are normally mentioned on the container); with epoxy resins, the two components not being mixed together properly or in the right proportions; insufficient patience with the hardening period.

Tacks

These can be used for stretching textiles over frames or panels and for fixing cardboards and wooden pieces. Try to buy the copper variety to prevent rust staining.

Materials that can be used

The list below should not by any means be taken as complete. It is intended to provide ideas for collecting the kind of things which can provide the fascinating working materials for the exploration of collage.

Acorns

These should always be well dried before use. The crisp shell will respond well when polished with a little furniture cream; some varieties come up with warm browns and ochres. Oak apples can also be collected.

Animal teeth

These may sometimes be come across during walks in woods. The hard shiny enamel surfaces can provide an accent, or if there are enough of them they can be used in pattern making.

Bark

The bark from different trees can provide a useful range of texture to work with. From the deep rugged chunks from some conifers to the silvery skin of some of the birches; from the gnarled hardness of oak bark to the flaking of the plane tree. Make sure it is dry right through before use. Do not take bark from growing trees. Use only that from dead wood.

Beads

Many and attractive different types of clear and opaque beads can be come across in a haberdasher's or an old curio shop. They can be either stuck down or sewn on to a textile.

Beans

These come in a wide variety of shape, colour and size, ranging from the larger such as the broad and haricot, to the smaller such as mung. They will normally be bought quite dry and hardened through. After sticking down, a coat of varnish will bring up the colours.

Blotting paper

It is worth having a sheet or two around as some pleasant soft bleeding effects with watercolour can be achieved on it and when cut out could provide just the special note that was being sought.

Bolts

A collection of these can provide good material if working in a bold manner on a heavy wooden support or sheet of metal. The smaller ones will probably stick satisfactorily with a synthetic glue, but large heavy ones may have to be wired into the support. Possible sources include old one-man garages, small fishing village shipyards, rambling country town ironmongers.

Bones from large animals

The butcher can nearly always come up with supplies for a reasonable sum, particularly if warned in advance. If the bones are moist and still have flesh and muscle on them they will have to be well boiled for several hours to get them stripped and clean. There is scope for experiment with some of the larger ones; try engraving into them with a knife blade or sharpened nail. The design can then be filled with a dark pigment. Bones that fit together in a skeleton can be arranged still interlocked at a fresh angle and against a striking background.

Bottle tops

Whether of the soft metal from milk bottles or the harder types from sauce bottles, these can be material for building into a form of mosaic pattern.

Braids, brocades and embroidered fragments

Bits and pieces of these may sometimes be discovered in some ancient work-basket, at jumble sales or begged from a small town dress shop. The rich materials from which they are made have many uses and provide focal points or strong brightly coloured accents.

Broken china and earthenware

Keep a box devoted to these materials. Whether of a hard glazed variety, brown earth or the red of flower pots, these forgotten fragments can be given a new term of use by being put into areas of mosaic or built into a mixed *assemblage* or one of many experiments with texture and form.

Buttons

The range here can seem almost endless, from the shining mother-of-pearl to the many horn examples, from metal to wood, from material-covered buttons to porcelain, from glass to bone, and the teeming mass of plastic buttons that are replacing the older ones. Some, such as mother-of-pearl, will need a little care if they are being stuck down because not all glues will take to them. The safest course is to try a few experiments with different types of adhesive, first making sure that the buttons are quite clean and degreased.

Cards and cardboard

For many these two are the basics for work. The thicker cardboards can act as supports, while the others and the cards can be built up to make reliefs. Both will stick down happily with most glues whether natural or synthetic. Perhaps one of the simplest to use with them is the PVA. Sources for collection are legion. Scrounge around shops such as grocers who are often only too pleased to be relieved of a rubbish disposal problem. Bookshops, ironmongers, printers, stationers are other places to look. Both cards and cardboards are where possible best cut with a sharp knife against a good hard straight edge. To protect the surface you are cutting on, put several layers of newspaper underneath the card; this will also give a slight springiness and allow the blade of the knife to penetrate right through the card or cardboard.

Carpets

Fragments of these can give an unexpected depth of texture often combined with rich colours and floral or abstract designs that can be placed into a growing composition. PVA will probably stick the coarse-grained material. Furniture shops and those dealing with the laying of carpets can be approached for waste material.

Catalogues, advertisements, tickets and other printed ephemera

Make sure that the examples chosen to work with have little value, as some of these things are rising in the opinion of specialist collectors. Such little mementoes pasted down in certain settings can often lend a note of interest. As most of them will be printed on wood pulp or probably esparto grass paper they will be liable to yellow and become brittle. To a degree both these conditions can be remedied by brushing them over with an acrylic medium broken with water in a ratio of one part acrylic to four parts water. A number of the acrylic media have an ultra-violet inhibiting agent combined with them which will retard the yellowing process.

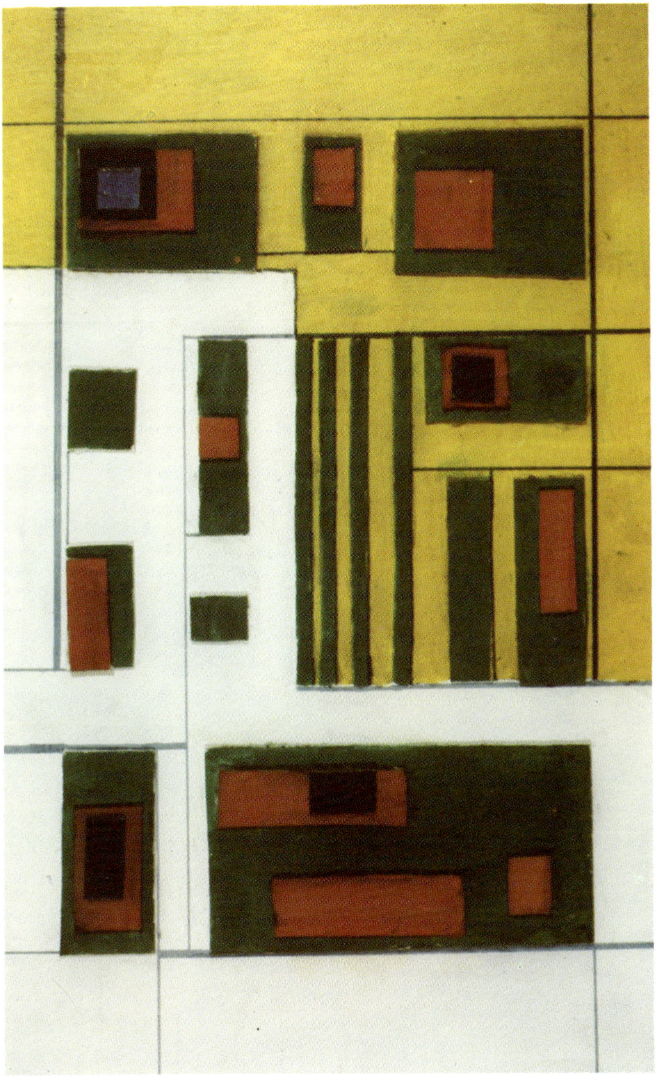

Coloured relief with cardboards

Cellophane

This and other plastic clear sheeting can have a number of uses. It can be coloured or have other sheet materials stuck to it with PVA. It can then perhaps be stretched on some small frame and fixed so that the sheet is suspended about half an inch clear of the support, thus giving a sense of another dimension.

Cereals

Breakfast cereals left whole or broken up fine, barley kernels and others of the same group all make useful materials for texture building. They may be laid into almost any of the glues depending on the idea and support.

Cheesecloth and muslin

Both versatile materials, these can be either used dry in their natural condition or moistened and sprinkled with plaster of Paris and quickly formed into folds or other designs before they harden.

Chicken wire

Whether of fine or coarse mesh this may be incorporated as another texture or it will provide strength for reinforcing *papier mâché* or plasters in relief.

Coffee grounds and tea leaves

It doesn't really matter whether these have been used for drinks or not, as long as they are dry. Brush on some adhesive and sprinkle down the grounds or leaves, and here are two more different-looking textures.

Cogs

There have been some fascinating experiments with these little and not so little toothed wheels. Where to find supplies? A polite word to a friendly watchmaker, a query to an engineering workshop, or a search through a long forgotten biscuit tin in the garage. Epoxy glues will serve best for sticking down.

Cones

A walk through a wood can often provide a variety of these strange little forms. There is an interesting contrast between the opened ones and the shut.

Cork

Whether from bottles or as pieces slung up by the tide, cork is worth considering. It will carve or cut quite easily to shape. It can also be chopped up to provide a coarse grounding material.

Corn grains

Jars of grains such as oats, wheat, maize, and barley are standbys that can have many uses.

Corrugated paper

This is one of the most interesting of the wrapping papers as it has this definite ridged look. Cutting it to shape needs care if the little ridges are not to be bruised. Possibly the best tool is the scalpel.

Cotton, thread and wool

These are all serviceable materials for making lines. Most glues will work satisfactorily; they should be brushed over the area to be worked and allowed to go tacky and then the strands should be pressed into position.

Cotton wool

This is a useful item for some areas but a difficult one to preserve. Spraying at short intervals with a mixture of one part acrylic medium to four parts water may serve to help hold it together, or a medium strong starch can be tried. The spray should be as fine as possible. The material can be stuck down with almost any of the glues.

Crayons

A form of somewhat original mosaic can be produced with small pieces of broken wax crayons. A metal sheet and heat are required and the fragments can be manoeuvred.

Crêpe paper

Although it has an intriguing surface look crêpe paper should be treated with care as most glues will soak through it, particularly water soluble ones which can also make the colours run. For success, try brushing down a thin layer of PVA and when nearly dry press the crêpe paper on to it.

Doilies

These are machine-cut plate decorations in white, gold, silver and sometimes other colours. Possibilities for use include cutting up to simulate lace fragments, folding into segments and pasting down whole as a foundation for later work.

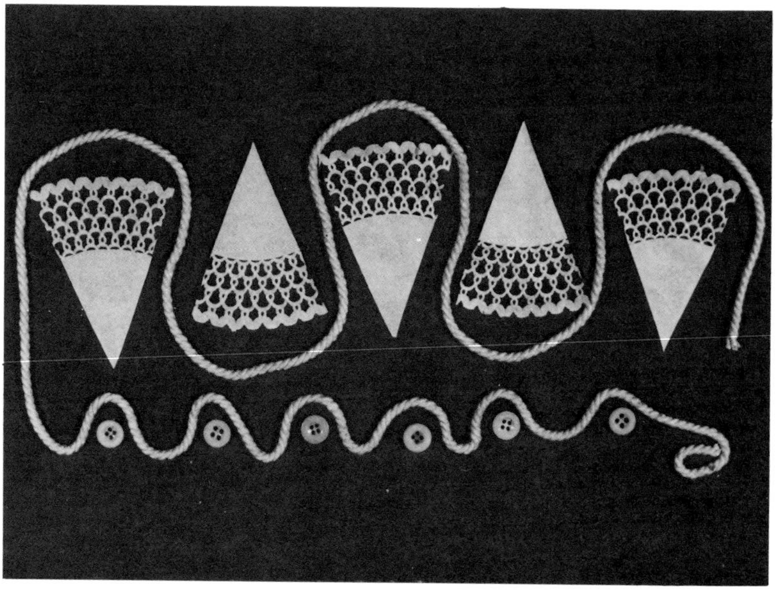

Doilies, cord and buttons

Dowelling

These wooden rods that come in sizes from about 5 mm ($\frac{1}{5}$ in) up to around 25 mm (1 in) can provide good dividers between colours and textures in an abstract composition. They may also be cut into short varied lengths and stuck down vertically to produce an unusual relief effect.

Dried berries, flowers, leaves and seedpods

The variety of these that can be collected and treated during the late summer and early autumn allows for building up stocks of materials that can spark off many imaginative ideas. Once the flowers are dried they are best stored in loose fitting plastic bags with ventilation holes and hung up. Fragile specimens of flowers, grasses and leaves can be strengthened by dipping in a solution of one part acrylic to five of water and then hung in the open air to dry off as soon as possible. PVA is perhaps the most satisfactory adhesive for fixing in place, particularly as it should harden out clear.

Drinking straws

The waxed paper or plastic types will both serve as line makers or they may be chopped up into short sections and built up with other small things as a form of mosaic or a variation of texture.

Dry pigments

These may be mixed with the adhesives to make a form of paint. They can also be put with such as whiting, marble dust or sand to create coloured modelling pastes. Another more subtle use is to first lightly spray an area with a one to one acrylic medium and water mixture and then dust the dry pigments on to the moist area. When dry, the excess can be blown or shaken away; the result being that a soft blush of the colour is left.

Eggshells

Crushed up and in PVA or acrylic medium, these can provide areas of speckled texture. They should be washed out before use.

Feathers

A country walk can often provide a selection of feathers; for the city dweller, a visit to a local dealer in game should produce a variety, especially in the winter. Delicate feathers can be strengthened in the same way as suggested for plant forms.

Ferns

The leaves are best dried by arranging them flat between two sheets of blotting paper and weighting them down.

Fish bones

Backbones from flatfish in particular are good pattern makers. The bones will generally dye with transparent colours such as crimson, some of the blues and greens. They can be varnished and then set in PVA.

Flex

This is useful for making swirling lines. If there is difficulty in getting it to stick down, moisten a piece of cotton wool with methylated spirit and draw the flex through to wipe off any grease.

Fur fragments

These materials can give unexpected effects; they should be set down with a contact adhesive that can be used for leather; PVA can also be used.

Glass

In small pieces glass will work in with a mosaic. An unusual effect can be achieved by placing a small pane of glass into position with PVA underneath and a thin coat on top. When it is dry, wrap a cloth around the hand and gently thump the glass with the handle of the hammer to cause a star break. Soak a piece of cotton wool in a strong tinting colour such as cadmium red and wipe over the starred glass forcing the colour into the cracks, lastly wiping the surface clean.

Gravels and pebbles

These can be collected from the banks or courses of brooks and streams and the seashore. Apart from colour, the main difference between the two is that the freshwater ones will tend to be sharper than the well smoothed kinds from the shore. Varnishing will bring up and hold the colours.

Lace

Fragments of lace can be strengthened by soaking in a one to three acrylic and water solution. To stiffen to a shape, use weak size or starch.

Leather

An interesting material to experiment with, leather may be dyed, painted on with acrylics, polished and tooled. Watch that you use a suitable adhesive. Some contact glues will serve but should state the fact on the container.

Lino

Small pieces of lino can be included in mosaic work or a design can be cut out and either left plain or filled with a paste. Most adhesives will adhere satisfactorily to the rough hessian backing, but it is wise to leave the pieces weighted for several hours to ensure they are fast.

Metal foils, rings, sheets and washers

Some contact glues will be able to hold such things fast, but for permanent work the epoxies are better. The main point is to be sure that all the surfaces have been thoroughly degreased. Scrapyards and small engineering works can often have useful-looking waste.

Moss

When looked for, a surprising amount of different types can be found, from small dense clumps with minute forms to the rough straggling variety that

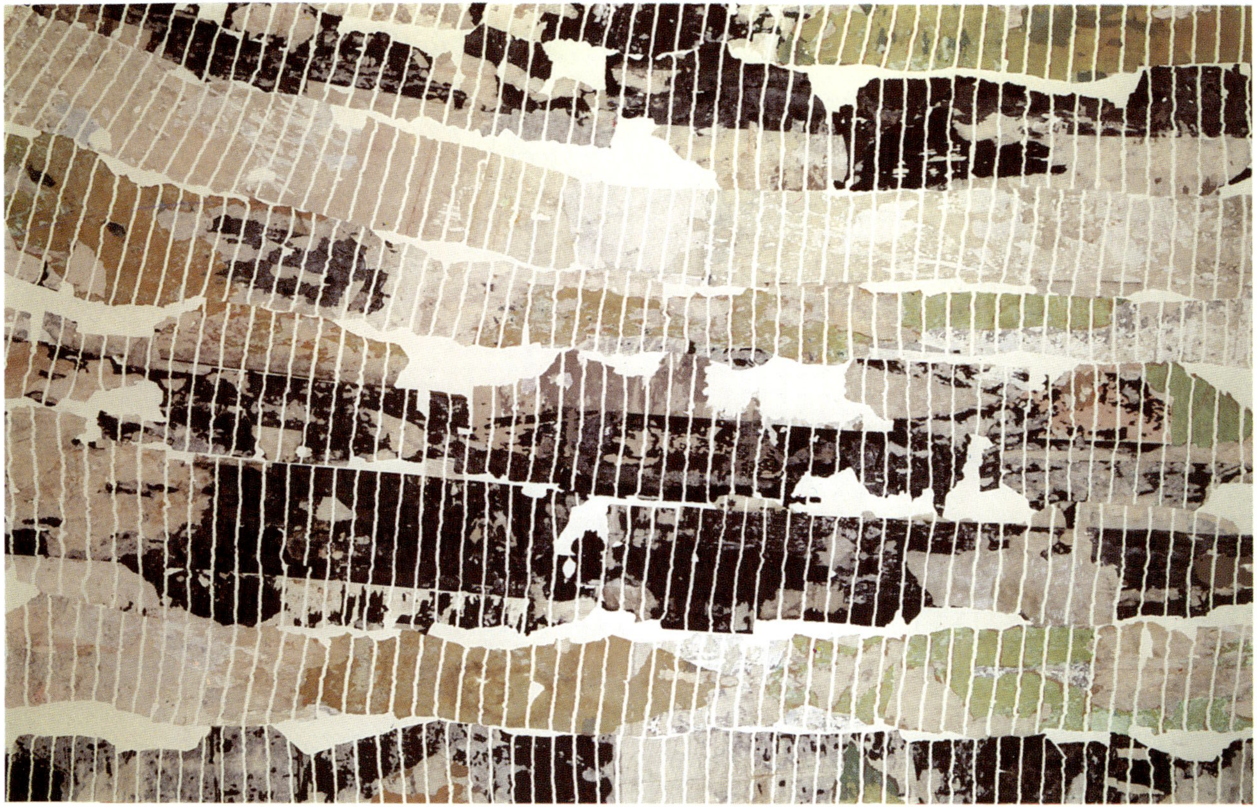

Gwyther Irwin, *Lazalo* (*Courtesy of Gimpel Fils*). Paper collage

sometimes grows round the boles of trees. It should be well dried out and will need quite a lot of adhesive; PVA is probably the most suitable.

Moulded plastics

Many kinds can be collected and stored away, such as packing sheets for fruit, egg boxes, plates and containers. Most will adhere satisfactorily if a contact that states it is for plastics is used.

Nails

These, apart from being used for fixing, can be interestingly employed to build up patterns in a composition. They are best set into an epoxy.

Papers

Keep an eye open for coloured tissues, graph papers, greaseproof, magazines, marbled paper, music sheets, newspapers, posters, sandpaper, paper towels, wallpaper and wrapping paper. Fragile papers such as tissue can be strengthened by brushing over with a one to three acrylic medium and water solution. Once papers have been set into the design they can be varnished or wax polished.

Paints

Any type may be incorporated, each adding its special characteristics. As was mentioned in the previous section, acrylics will also serve as an adhesive. In fact they are probably the most versatile and useful to work with in collage because they can be applied very stiff or diluted, to most substances which, provided they are not greasy, will bond with the colours.

Pastas

A look down the shelves of a supermarket can generally reveal a large variety: spaghetti, macaroni, vermicelli and numerous little strange shapes made from the pasta. All of these will set well in PVA or the contacts. It is wiser not to use a water-soluble natural glue, for this could make the pasta swell and distort.

Plastic sponges and foam

These can be shaped up by tearing or cutting with a scalpel. Suitable contact glues will set them in place.

Powders

Modelling pastes can be made from such as kaolin, marble dust, sand,

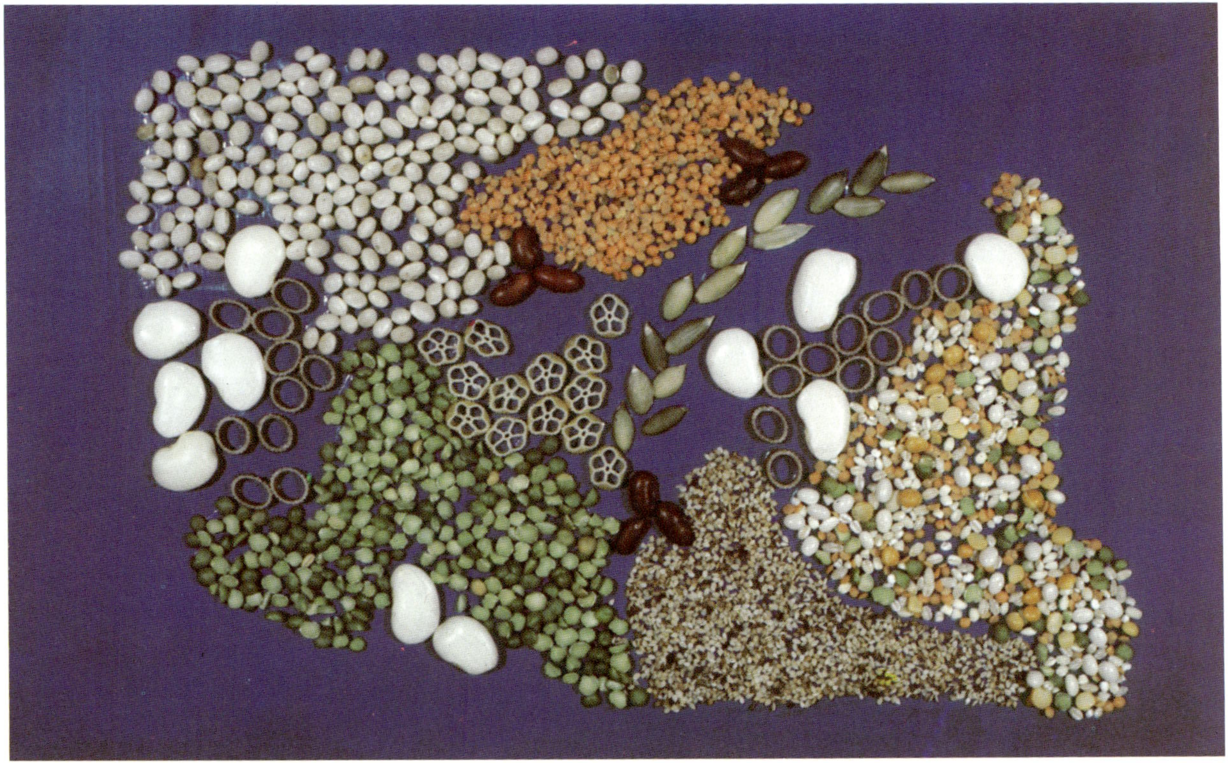

Grain, pasta and seeds

sawdust and whiting. They can be mixed with a one to three acrylic medium and water solution or with PVA and water in the same proportions. Colouring can be added with dry powder colours or acrylic paints. There are a number of commercial powders and pastes that will also serve. Plaster of Paris could be included in the stock.

Ribbons

The choice can range from narrow strips of velvet ribbon to three inch wide satins, from frail silks to fancy patterned. They are probably best set with PVA but care should be taken that not too much is applied as it will soak through and cause unsightly blemishes.

Rope, cord and string

These are all useful to add lines and swirling forms. They can be fixed with contacts, epoxies or PVA. They are best cut with a very sharp knife or scalpel to prevent the cut ends from fraying out. If a particularly thick rope tends to fray, even when cut with the sharpest knife, the area around where the cut is to be made can be soaked with a solution of one part acrylic and three parts water. Allow to dry and you should get a fray-proof end section.

Sequins

These have been somewhat neglected, yet they hold exciting possibilities with their glitter and colour; if displayed in movement or with a moving light, a sparkling and unusual sensation can be created. Contact glues fix them satisfactorily or if working on a textile they can be sewn into place.

Shavings

Both wood and metal shavings have places in some designs. The wood will stick with contact and the metal with epoxy.

Shore things

Take a shopping bag down to the beach and there is a wealth of strange items that can be picked up and that are just begging to be used with collage. Look carefully and any of the following can be collected: shells, discarded crab shells, seaweeds, sea-smoothed and contorted driftwood, whitened bones; all of which should be washed in fresh water and allowed to dry before use. Tiny shells were a great favourite when our mid nineteenth-century ancestors were preparing loving greeting cards. Some of the more fragile seaweeds can be set on to glass with PVA or acrylic medium, after which they can be incorporated in the main design and can add an unusual feature.

Slate

As this will split fairly easily, flakes can be produced for use in relief work. They will set with most contacts or epoxies. Further treatment can include painting, waxing and varnishing.

Small cardboard boxes and tins

Often useful to add as a feature or point of interest these are best kept below 100 mm (4 in) in length or breadth and 25 mm (1 in) in height. Cardboard varieties will stick down with contact, and metal, after being degreased, with epoxy. Often the printed or pictorial matter displayed can be used to advantage.

Stamps

The common and current ones can be soaked off and will provide interesting material for mosaic work, either left whole or cut up into miniature tesserae. PVA, water-soluble pastes or contacts will set them down.

Stone fragments

A search round an old quarry can generally provide numerous interesting shapes from which ideas can grow. If you use a hammer to break them smaller, it is wise to wear some form of eye protection. Stone is best set in epoxy.

Straws

These were another favourite with our ancestors who would spend long hours building up intricate inlays with the golden stems of corn gathered up at harvest time. Contact glues will serve but they are probably best set into PVA; when dry the straws can be waxed or varnished.

Textiles

Most wool, cotton, or silk fabrics will take adhesives satisfactorily. Synthetic materials will not always and should be tested first with the selected glue. Be sure the colour does not run. The choice for collage is wide, and any of these will serve: denim, linen, oilcloth, satin, chiffon, taffeta, tweeds, scrim, dhootie, felts, net, and the list can be added to by a visit to a haberdasher's or a dress shop. The main point to watch when sticking textiles down is that not too much adhesive is used, for if it soaks through the material to the front it will spoil the effect. If doing appliqué, a little adhesive should be applied to the ground material and the back of the patch; this should be allowed to go tacky, and the patch should then be pressed into position.

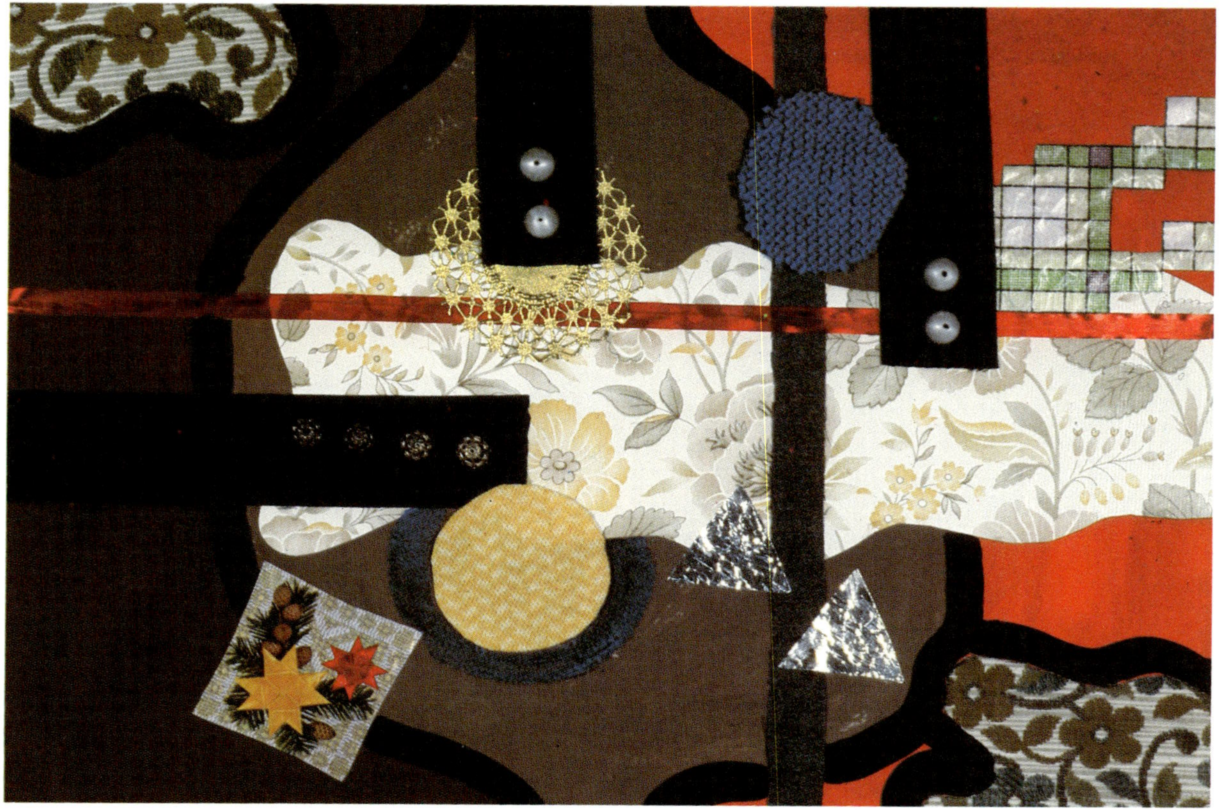

Mixed materials

Varnish

This can be useful for bringing up all or certain areas, and it can also serve to consolidate some fragile materials. The choice can vary between the water-clear synthetic varnishes and the natural resins such as mastic, dammar and copal. The latter generally has a warm yellow-brown tinge which can be attractive over woods. The clear synthetic may be tinged with oil colours, if an overall coloured veil is sought. Don't apply varnish to materials such as cotton wool, moss, feathers, dried plants or any textiles because the result will be a nasty soggy unsightly mess.

Waxes

Some have tried melting these on a heated metal plate and stirring dry pigments into them with spatulas and instruments like combs, which procedure has finally achieved an effect of marbling. It is an interesting idea that could be incorporated in certain projects. Paraffin wax can be used on most papers and cards to bring up resist effects, and beeswax will serve after being mixed with a little turpentine as a very effective polish for surfaces of wood, straw, some rocks and shells. If making up a polish, melt 50 g ($1\frac{3}{4}$ oz) of beeswax, and when liquid stir in 100 cc ($3\frac{1}{2}$ fl oz) of either real or substitute turpentine. This quantity can be increased or decreased to produce a creamier or stiffer polish as desired.

Wire

Copper or steel wire will come in useful, not only for securing some objects but also as line makers. If used for the latter, they should be set into epoxy.

Wood

Offcuts and scraps can usually be obtained from a friendly carpenter's shop or a woodyard. Fixing can be by nail, panel pin, screw or any of the glues. Finishing can be by polishing, varnishing or painting.

Supports

The most important point with regard to a support for collage is that it must be rigid. Any whipping and bending will tend to loosen the materials which have been stuck on. If a support does need strengthening, this should be done before work starts. Owing to the possibly fragile nature of a collage, once it is completed it is almost impossible to apply battens or backing to the reverse side.

There are a number of materials that are suitable to work on, each with their own characteristics. The choice will, to a degree, be decided by the type and size of collage envisaged. Whatever is selected, it is worth a little time preparing it, so that the completed collage will have the best chance of permanence.

Cardboards

The range is large, from fairly thin white cards up to strawboards around 5 mm ($\frac{1}{5}$ in) thick, and included under this heading are also fashion and Bristol boards averaging 3 mm ($\frac{1}{8}$ in) thick. For experimental work, recourse can be made to stout cardboard cartons from which satisfactory panels of up to about 500 mm by 380 mm (20 by 15 in) can be cut.

Thin white cards of about 1 mm ($\frac{1}{32}$ in) will only serve for small works up to around 150 mm (6 in) across. The heaviest strawboards should be all right unsupported to a size of around 600 mm by 500 mm (24 by 20 in). For larger sizes, or if the materials are on the heavy side, the strawboards can be stiffened by gluing wood battens to the back. If panel pins or small nails are also used, the heads should be isolated with shellac or a touch of epoxy to prevent rust staining through any work on the front.

As the surface of cardboards may be on the absorbent side, it is generally helpful to give them some priming. This can consist of a brushing over with size or a mixture of one part acrylic medium to four parts water. Alternatively a coat of a proprietory acrylic primer can be applied or a good quality white emulsion paint.

Hardboard

This is also known as masonite and comes in varying thicknesses up to about 4 mm ($\frac{1}{6}$ in) with different degrees of hardness. It is a very suitable support for collage, being smooth on the face side and having a weave mark on the reverse. Panels up to about 800 mm by 700 mm (30 by 27 in) should be safe without battening. The side to be worked on is best given some kind of priming, as suggested for strawboard. If using heavy materials it will help adhesion if the smooth surface is roughened with coarse sandpaper or crisscross scratched with a sharp point before priming.

Chipboard

This is a very strong man-made board; a thickness of around 14 mm ($\frac{1}{2}$ in) will give satisfactory panels of up to 2400 mm by 1200 mm (96 by 48 in). Priming and preparation can be as for hardboard. One small point with regard to hanging: chipboard is heavy and will need more than just screw eyes put into the back. The best course is first to fix a small wooden plate at each of the top corners; for strength use a glue as well as screws or nails. On to this plate fix two substantial metal shelf ears which can then be plugged into the wall.

Pulpboard

This is a soft man-made board that will be sufficiently rigid up to around 1200 mm by 900 mm (48 by 35 in). As it is highly absorbent, it will need a very thorough priming to make it a safe support for glued-on materials, but it is eminently suitable for use with textiles or papers that are to be attached by staples, pins or small tacks. The edges are particularly prone to fraying, so this should be guarded against by brushing them over with a hoof glue or a one to one mixture of acrylic medium and water or slightly diluted PVA.

Plywood

This may be three, five or seven ply and if it has been treated to resist woodworm it will make a reliable support. The thinner varieties will not need strengthening unless they are larger than around 800 mm by 600 mm (30 by 24 in), the thickest being safe up to 2400 mm by 1200 mm (96 by 48 in). Priming can be as for the other boards. One feature with plywood is that as it is prepared from slices of real timber the naked wood look can be incorporated in a design. It may be engraved, stained, waxed or varnished.

Wood panels

Unless it is envisaged that very heavy materials such as chunks of metal, rock and the like will be used, there is little point in going to the expense and trouble of preparing a panel. If, however, the work plan does call for strength, a panel can be put together from well-seasoned or kiln-dried deal. For sizes up to 800 mm by 600 mm (30 by 24 in) and working with timber of 25 mm (1 in) thick, it will be sufficient just to epoxy glue the planks together. For larger sizes, the backs of panels should be strengthened by battening. The working surface should be primed as before.

For some specialized subjects calling for an intense white hard ground a gesso can be applied. This traditional treatment can be prepared from dilute rabbit-skin glue and whiting. The consistency for the first coat, *gesso grosso*, should be like thick scalded cream. The finishing coat, *gesso sottile*, should be similar to single cream. The gessos should be brushed on as flat as possible. It often helps to gently tap round the edge of the panel with a hammer because the concussion waves will tend to level out the gesso. The panel should then be left to dry for 48 hours, and finally the surface should be smoothed over with fine sandpaper.

Textiles

The fabric chosen will have to be stretched on a frame or over a panel, or stuck down on to a panel. Even if it is decided that the collage is to hang free after being worked, it is still better to mount it temporarily. There is a wide choice of suitable materials which include unprimed artist's canvas, sailcloth, hessian, sacking, various linens, corduroy, denim, duck cloth, hopsack, various nets, poplin, towelling and velvet.

The simplest answer for a frame is to purchase a stretcher that is used for painting-canvas. It is important to line up the sides of the stretcher so that they are parallel with the threads of the weave; if they are not, distortion can easily take place. Having done this, stand the stretcher on end and place the chosen fabric over it so that there will be enough for a lap of about 40 mm over on to the back. Now put in a copper tack or copper-plated staple in the middle of this side, turn the stretcher over and repeat, turn on to the side and repeat once more, turn again and put in the fourth tack or staple. After this, work towards one corner at a time, and lastly, if it is to be permanent, lay the stretched fabric face down and fix the lap all round the back. If the collage is to be dismounted after working, it is best just to fix it round the edge with staples rather than tacks, as the former can be more easily removed by prising out with a screwdriver.

Textiles can be mounted on small sheets of thick strawboard or, for larger sizes, on hardboard, pulpboard or chipboard; a suitable adhesive is either acrylic medium or PVA. In both cases take care the adhesive does not soak through to the front of the fabric. The most satisfactory procedure is to brush a thin coat of the adhesive on to both the panel and the fabric; allow these to get tacky—this usually takes about ten minutes—then place the fabric down on the panel and smooth into position with the hands or with the help of a roller.

If the collage is to be hung when finished, it may need some support in the way of a dowelling rod fitted into a hem along the top and a similar one at the bottom. If extra weight is needed to get a satisfactory hang, small fishing weights may be sewn in at intervals, or a lead wire wound round the dowel before it is placed in the hem.

Whether or not the fabric will need an overall dressing will depend on the type chosen. If it is felt that one is needed, a mixture of one part acrylic medium to four parts water will serve well with such as canvas, sailcloth, hessian, sacking, linen, duck, hopsack and poplin.

Glass

There have been some attractive designs worked out with a form of collage on sheets of glass. These have been intended to be displayed so that the full effect of transparent materials can be glimpsed. For this approach the glass should be fairly thick to give strength and should be mounted let into a frame. The only preparation needed is to be sure that the glass is clean and thoroughly degreased; the simplest way to do this is to wipe it over with a small piece of soft rag which has been dipped in methylated spirit.

Metal sheets

The most suitable metal sheets are of zinc, aluminium or copper. Steel, except in very small sizes, is going to be too heavy. It is easiest to get the supplier to cut the size needed. It is best to have the sheets mounted on to wooden frames. To do this, bend the sheet over the edges and round to the back so that it can be fastened down from there, as it doesn't help to have a line of nail or screw heads showing round the front.

Walls

There is no reason why collage should not be carried out as a mural. The main point is to be certain that the wall is in a condition to take the work. To prepare the wall, first brush on a mixture of equal parts acrylic medium and water; this will serve to consolidate the surface if it is at all loose. When this coat has dried, feel to see if the surface is now sound; if not, apply a second coat. Finally, if desired there can be a finishing coat of acrylic primer. On to this surface, work can be carried out in any materials that are suitable and in sympathy with the support. At the finish, if there are no textiles or over-absorbent materials in the composition, the surface can be strengthened with an overall coat of glossy or matt acrylic medium.

Procedures and techniques

Appliqué

If patches of fabric are not to be sewn on to the base material the best adhesive to use is PVA. It is important not to soak the fabric with glue as it will come through and mark the front surface. Put a light application on to the back of the patch and also on the base material, allow to get tacky and then bring the two together with moderate pressure. The natural water-soluble glues are not suitable, but watered down to a size consistency they will serve to strengthen and stiffen fabrics.

Blistering

Most of the oil- and emulsion-bound paints, whether for artists or decorators, will blister if heated. If this treatment is used with care, some interesting

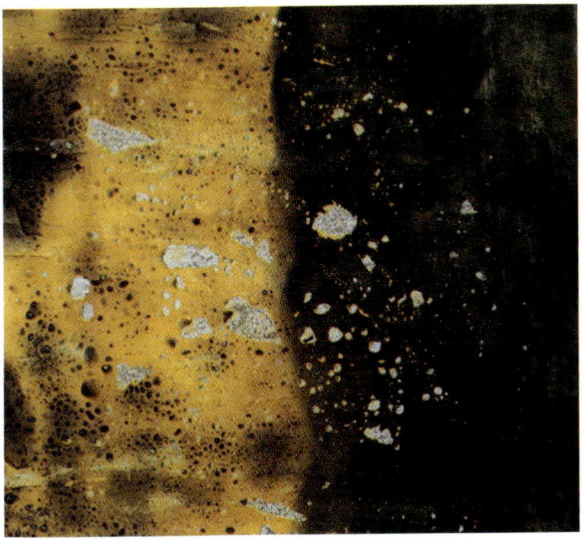

Scorching and blistering paint

textures can be produced. The paint to be treated should be applied to a firm support such as hardboard, plywood, chipboard or a wooden panel. For the most satisfactory result it should be brushed out to an even thickness overall. The actual applying of the heat is best done out-of-doors because of fire hazard and also as there will probably be quite heavy clouds of rather obnoxious smoke. The easiest and most controllable method of heating is to use a small butane cylinder blowlamp. These have a valve which controls the size of the flame, from a broad sweep down to a needle point. Start with a medium flame and keep it moving over the whole area to be treated. The paint surface will very soon start to bubble up and the process can be stopped when the desired effect has been reached.

With care it is possible to bring up the blistering and still keep some of the colour. The area can be left as it is or, after cooling, the tops of the blisters can be crushed and the broken paint swept away. This will leave a rather strange cratered appearance which can be varnished if desired.

Cardboard relief

Depending on the size of the work planned the support may be thick strawboard for small to medium sizes, and after that hardboard or chipboard. Any of the adhesives mentioned will serve, but if using water soluble ones from the glue-pot do not be too liberal, because if you are the absorbent cardboards may buckle.

Working in this way contrasts can be achieved not only by shape and the thicknesses of the boards used but also by their texture. This can range from the 'hot-pressed' surfaces of the thin cards to the 'rough' and 'not' of the Bristol boards and the broken feel of the heavier straw and pulp boards.

When planning the design, cut out the pieces to be applied and then spend some time moving them around, working out the most satisfying arrangement. When doing the actual gluing, be careful that there is no spillage or excess that can be squeezed out and spoil the effect.

Cardboard reliefs can be left as they are or they may be painted or brushed over with weak gesso or plaster of Paris. Once the material has hardened, it can be trimmed up with fine sandpaper. Various panels of the design may also be engraved and filled.

Collograph

This is the name for a print that can be taken from a certain type of collage. It is a method that opens up exciting possibilities for experiments with the unusual and sometimes dramatic. Depending on the way that the collage block is built up the print can be taken either by the relief or intaglio process.

A start can be made with a piece of hardboard of any convenient size. It is best to use the smooth side and on to this stick objects such as dried leaves, flat fish bones, wire paperclips, lengths of string, fine gravel, sawdust, sand, thin metal washers, pieces of coarsely woven material such as muslin, cheesecloth, hessian and sacking, and small strips of wood. Try to pick objects of about the same thickness. After the whole has hardened out, to help when inking, the surface should be brushed over with a mixture of equal parts acrylic medium and water.

Suitable printing papers include tissues, greaseproof, shelf, newsprint and thin cartridge. To take a relief print rub up some black oil colour on a piece of glass with the roller and then carefully go over the face of the collage block so that only the upstanding parts receive the ink. After that, place the printing paper down on to the block; it may be damped to produce a softer line print. Smooth over with the hand and apply some pressure with a clean roller or with the back of a spoon. Then lift off the paper by picking up one end.

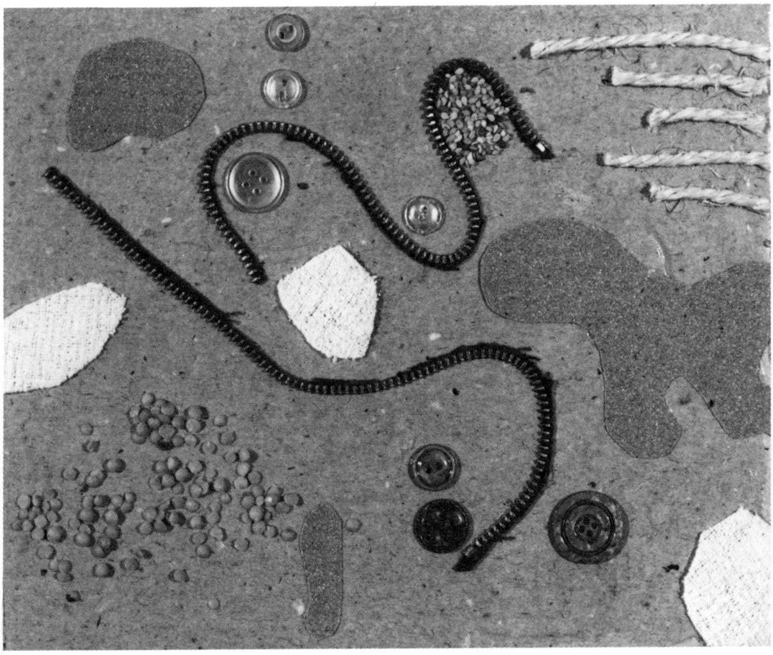

Collograph block

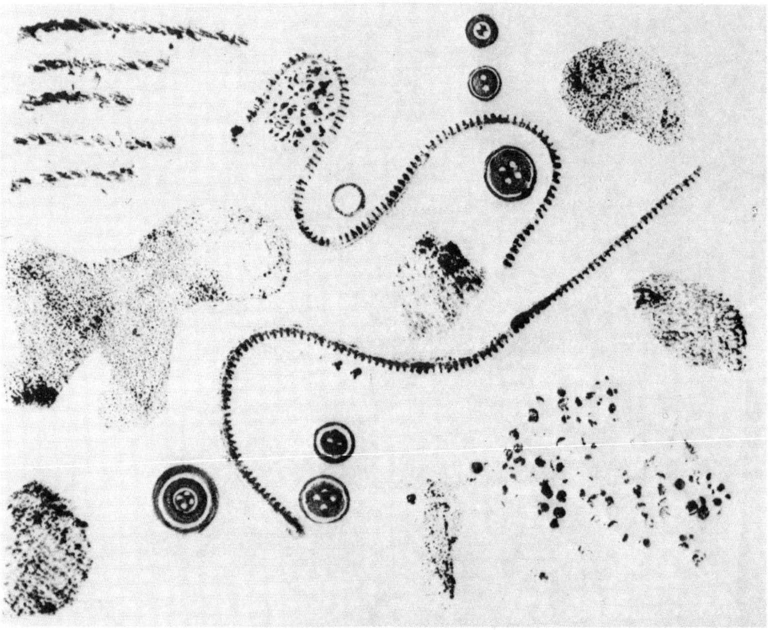

Print from collograph block

To take an intaglio print, make up a dabber with a piece of cotton wool inside some clean rags. Pick up some ink and go over the block dabbing the ink down into the area between the objects stuck on. Be patient with this, working the ink right into the gaps between fishbones, gravel and the like. Having done that, with another piece of clean rag work over the block and carefully clear away any ink that has got on to the upstanding faces of the objects. When taking the print it is best to always slightly dampen the printing paper as this will allow it to be forced down into the block face. After the paper has been put into position, go over it with another piece of cotton wool and a rag dabber and if necessary in certain areas work down with the fingertips. Finally lift up the print as with the relief. Dampened blotting paper can sometimes be used successfully with the intaglio method.

Printing may also be tried using acrylic colours, gouache or powder colours mixed to the right consistency with size or paste.

Drapes

Amusing and interesting effects can be achieved by preparing a fair-sized bowl of weak plaster of Paris, about the consistency of double cream. Into this can be dipped thin materials such as cheesecloth, muslin, net, poplin, cottons and the like. These can then be lifted out and arranged with draped folds on a support. All manner of patterns can be developed, being manipulated either with the finger or small pieces of smooth-ended dowel rod.

Drawing and cutting out shapes

All designs in paper, card or textiles should be drawn out and cut to shape before they are placed in position. If an attempt is made to alter a fragment already in place it is unlikely to succeed and may disturb adjacent materials.

It is generally desirable to have as clean-cut edges as possible. The easiest way to achieve this with papers and cards is to use a scalpel. Place half a dozen sheets of newspaper on top of an old piece of hardboard. Lay the material to be cut on top of this and work along a straight edge for ruled lines; for curves, try to keep the scalpel moving as smoothly as possible. Fabrics are best cut with scissors with the possible exception of felts and carpet pieces which are more suited to the edge of a modelling knife or scalpel.

Frottage

Although this is not a collage method in itself, the results produced from it can be useful material for inclusion in some compositions. The name frottage just means the taking of a rubbing from some textured or modelled surface. This can be done using a soft pencil or large fat wax crayon, and fairly thin papers that have enough give in them to slightly sink into the face of the object being rubbed.

Materials that are suitable for taking rubbings from include the surfaces of sawn timbers, dried leaves, fishbones, coarse canvas, hessian, sacking, coins, small keys, corrugated paper, chicken wire, flat undressed stone surfaces, fragments of incised lettering, engraved and etched tablets, and in fact almost anything that has a flat surface with a texture in it. Max Ernst was one of the early Surrealists who explored the taking of rubbings and introduced them into his collage work, sometimes combined with painting techniques.

A second use for frottage in the context of collage work is to take a rubbing from a finished collage, provided the face of the design is not too rugged. This is more successful when the materials are of a firm quality and more or less of the same thickness. The paper on which the rubbing is to be taken should be secured round the back of the collage with adhesive tape to prevent movement. A variation to this can be to take several repetitive rubbings of the same composition. After the first rubbing, free the paper and slightly move it along, secure once more and take the second rubbing;

repeat this process as many times as desired. With some pictures this can induce an impression of movement rather in the manner of *Dog on a Leash* painted in 1912 by Giacomo Balla (1871–1958), a member of the Italian Futurist Movement.

Gold and other metallic powders

The gold is not genuine but is prepared, like the other metallic powders, from bronze or brass alloys which can be made to simulate a number of metals. They can also be tinted blue, red, crimson, green, ochre and purple, all of which will come up with a metallic sheen. These powders can be mixed with acrylic medium and floated on to a specific area. Then, whilst they are still fluid they may be manipulated with combs and small rods to simulate a form of marbling. They can also be mixed into epoxy adhesives, varnishes and acrylic medium. It should be noted that even when imprisoned away from the air with glues or varnishes, these bronze powders will tend to darken and discolour.

Gold leaf

This fragile and costly material can serve to give highlights to a composition. It should only be laid on a surface that is firm enough to support it: gesso, isolated cards and cardboards and some base metals. The adhesive best suited is acrylic medium. One imaginative use of gold leaf has been developed by the Irish artist Patrick Scott. The support he uses is a raw canvas woven from local Balbriggan flax. First a coat of acrylic gloss medium is laid on to the canvas. This is allowed to dry and then a second coat is brushed on. After this has dried a third coat is applied and when this is tacky the gold leaf is laid directly into it. When all this has hardened a final coat of gloss acrylic medium will provide an enrichment.

To handle the extremely thin gold leaf successfully a special wide soft hair brush is needed which is called a 'tip'. To further enrich the appearance of the gold a preliminary coat of gold ochre or a warm red-brown such as burnt sienna can be applied.

Metal foils

These comparatively thin sheets can be of aluminium and sometimes of zinc and they can be used to give quite impressive surface facings. A design can be built up with plaster of Paris or stiff gesso, modelled and engraved and allowed to dry. When thoroughly hard, brush over the surface with a contact glue for metal, or an epoxy, and then lay a sheet of foil over the whole, folding the edges over to the back. Whilst the adhesive is still malleable, using fingers, fingernails and soft-nosed instruments that will

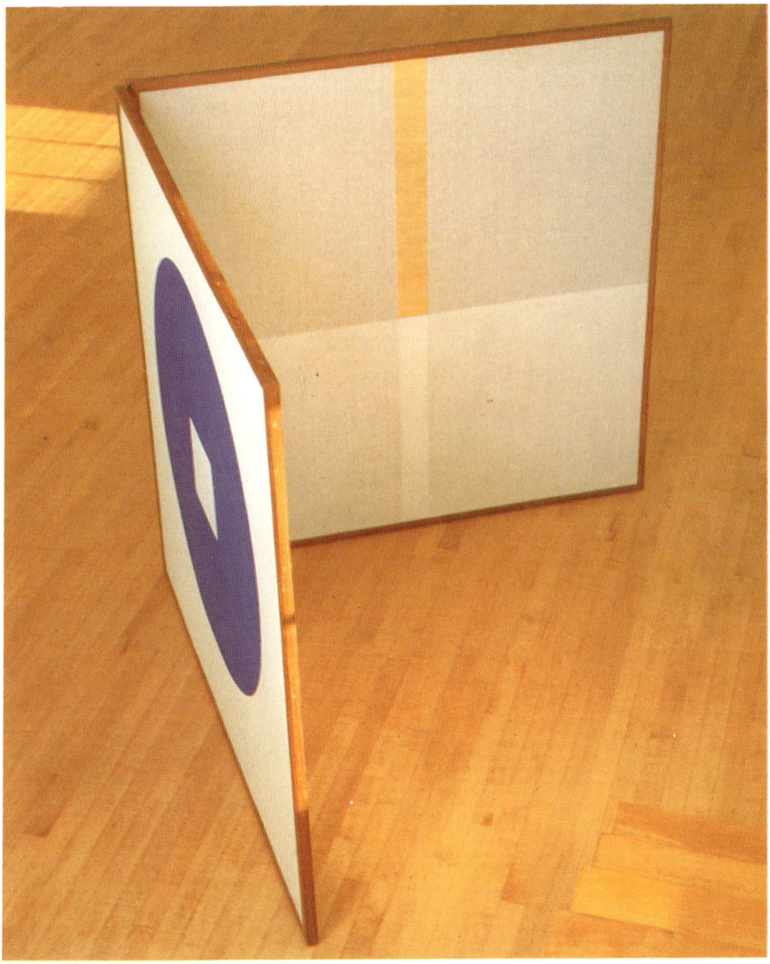

Patrick Scott: diptych (*Courtesy of Annely Juda Fine Art, London*). Raw canvas stretched and stuck on to a hardboard panel with gold leaf and acrylic colour application

not damage the foil, work it into the features of the design underneath. Final surface treatment can be to brush a little dark colour—burnt umber is suitable—over the whole and then wipe off most of it aiming to leave a subtle veil over all except for the highlights. Some of the colour can be worked into the deep cracks and crevices.

A different treatment is to work into the surface of the foil with combs, dies and other instruments to build up texture.

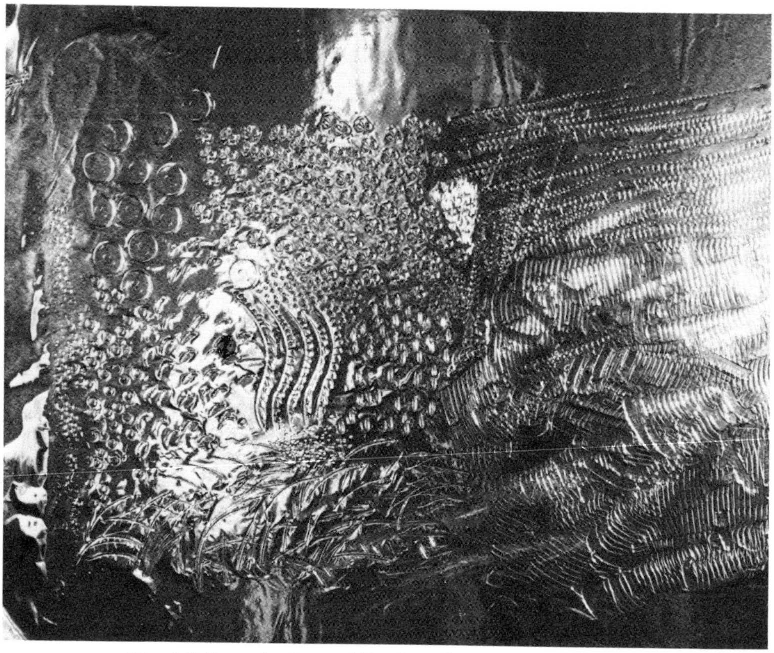

Metal foil, worked on while the adhesive was still moist

Metals

Whichever ones are used, don't overlook the effects of tarnish and rust. To a degree the action of these can be curtailed by applying a suitable lacquer. Some of the contact glues will serve, as will the epoxy, but it is best to experiment first to be sure of results.

Montage

Basically this is a method of picture-making using fragments of existing pictures such as photographs and pages of illustrative material from magazines. The pieces can be laid alongside each other or be superimposed. Flour paste, proprietary pastes, size, PVA and some contacts are all suitable. Apart from these, all that is needed for an instructive and often amusing exploration is a sheet of stiff card or strawboard, a sharp pair of scissors and an inquisitive and exploring eye. There is almost unlimited scope. The placing of often incongruous images alongside each other can trigger off all kinds of imaginative pursuits.

Mosaic

The support for this type of work needs to be quite firm, at the least thick

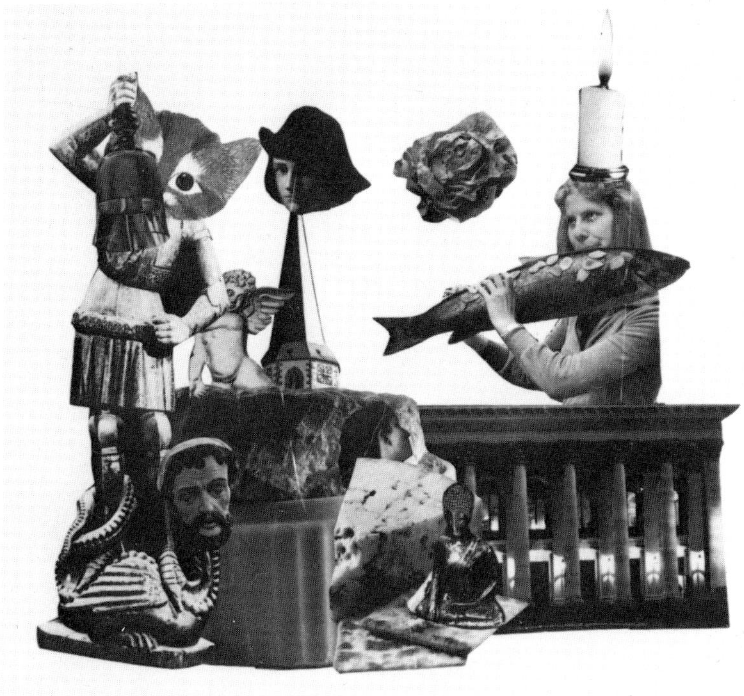

Photomontage

strawboard, but better still hardboard and for large scale work it should be chipboard. The materials suitable for tesserae can include shards of ceramics and glass, seeds, gravel and pebbles, small sections of dowel and other wooden rods, sea shells, whole or broken, torn or cut-up pieces of plain or coloured papers, cut-up cards and cardboards and small buttons. They can be set directly into PVA or acrylic medium. A second method is to prepare a paste of marble dust, kaolin, or whiting with PVA or acrylic medium; trowel this over the area to be treated and then push the pieces firmly into this. When the whole has hardened out, whichever way has been used, it can be given a surface coat of varnish or wax polish.

Plain paper

Don't ignore the simplicity of just using plain white or tinted papers; often from such an economical source a satisfying harmony can be produced. The joins of the various paper shapes can perhaps be marked with ruled coloured lines or separated with low walls of wire, straws or threads.

Plant forms

The dried and pressed specimens that will have been collected are material that will provide many a useful texture or feature in any number of compositions, or they may be used all by themselves to make the whole picture. Probably one of the best adhesives for use with these is a matt acrylic medium which will hold well and be nearly invisible.

Printed ephemera

These reminders of yesterday can be built into a montage, used as points of interest or imaginatively combined in a composition. Try sticking them down on some tightly stretched fabric such as denim or green baize in a haphazard arrangement as might be seen on the noticeboard of a small hotel. The effect can be completed with a grid of diagonal pink tapes, with brass-headed tacks or drawing pins where the tapes cross. As these scraps of paper will have been made from grass or wood pulp they will yellow, so give them, as has been suggested, a coat of acrylic medium and water which will help to slow down the process.

Relief in depth

Although a maximum depth cannot be given exactly, a rough limit of around 60 mm ($2\frac{1}{2}$ in) should be kept to. Over this the picture is going to become unwieldy and prone to damage. But this depth does allow for considerable experimentation with a mass of materials. The choice can include lumps of wood, boxes, tins, packaging for eggs and fruit, metal waste, stones, large shells, bunched textiles, thick ropes, chain and large shards.

Bearing in mind the weight of the finished composition the support must be adequate. For pictures up to 600 mm by 500 mm (24 in by 20 in) hardboard is suitable; over that either battened hardboard or chipboard is required. For some of the heavier objects it may be better not to glue but to bind them to the support by threading wire through from the back, or to fix them by screwing down small strips of metal over some concealed part of the object. Where smaller pieces of metal or shards are being positioned it will be found that an epoxy will serve; for metal, use it quite liberally, so that it spreads over parts of the object. Wood, cardboard objects, rope and pulp packaging will stick with natural glues, textiles with PVA and other substances with specified contact glues.

A relief in depth can of course be an invitation to work with considerable freedom. Most of the other methods mentioned here can be included. Such manners as mosaic, blistering, montage, painting and foil work can all be

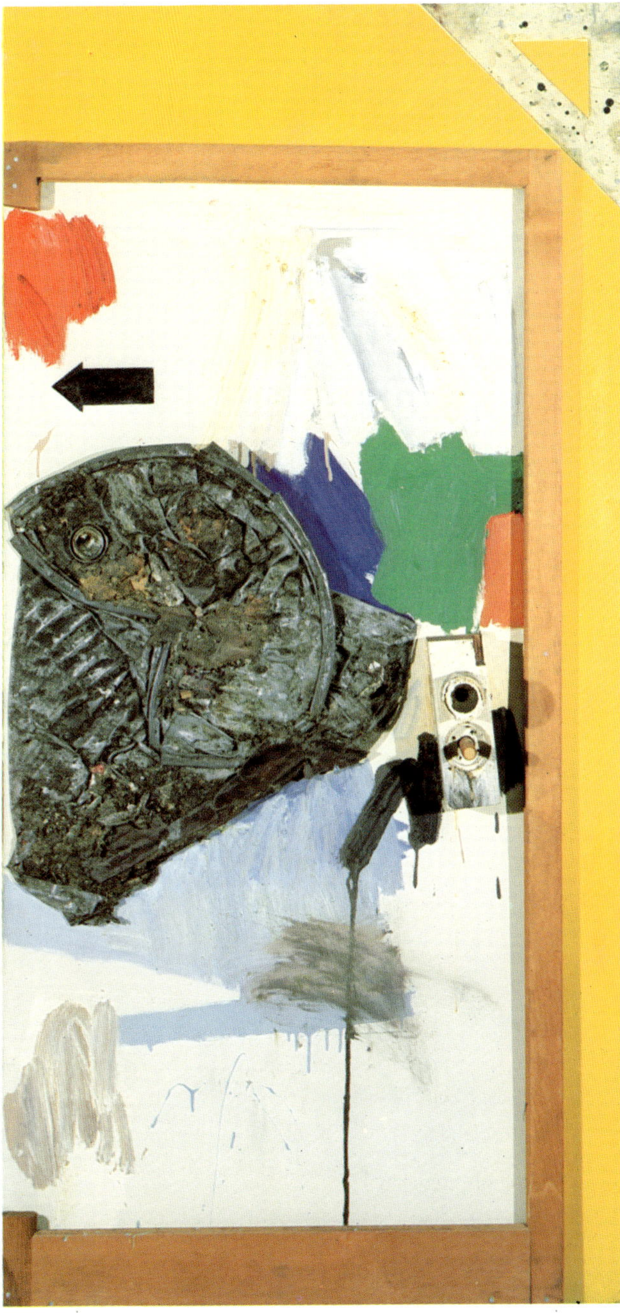

Robert Rauschenberg: Cartoon (*Courtesy of Christie's*)

exploited to add enrichment. Bear in mind that light and shade are particular factors with this approach and can greatly affect the final result.

Seed and grain work

Here again it is important that the support should be rigid; for small sizes up to about 400 mm by 300 mm (16 × 12 in), thick strawboard or panels cut from cardboard packing cases will serve; over that it should be hardboard or for still larger work, chipboard. The support may be left plain but many prefer to lay a ground colour. The reason for this is twofold. First, however tightly packed the seeds and grain are, there can be some ground left showing through, and if it has been left plain it can give the finished picture a bit of a thin look. Secondly, some seeds and grain such as barley, rice, pumpkin and others can tend to become slightly transparent once embedded in the glue.

Practically all the glues discussed with the exception of water pastes will serve with these small objects. PVA or acrylic medium are perhaps best because both of these should dry out completely transparent. The trick with

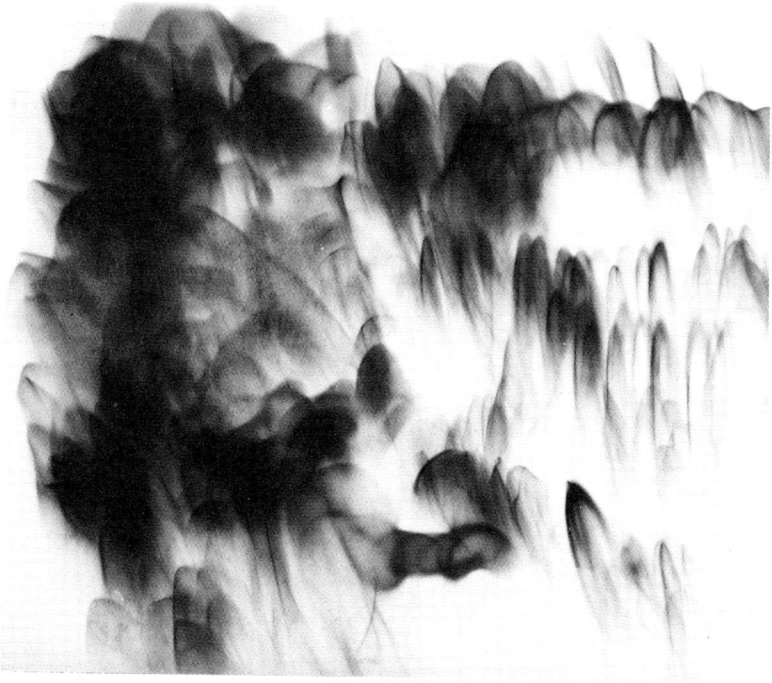

Smoking with tapers held at different angles

this technique, as with any in collage, is to use enough adhesive but not so much that it shows sufficiently to mar the composition.

Smoking

Areas of paper or card work can be given a subtle touch by holding the whole picture upside down over a small bundle of burning tallow tapers. The flames should not be allowed to touch any of the materials, only the thick oily smoke. This is not an easy process to control and some kind of masking should be worked out for the areas that are not intended to be smoked. Household decorators sell a serviceable self-adhesive masking tape about 25 mm (1 in) wide; this will hold quite firmly enough during the operation and afterwards will peel off without damaging the materials. It is possible to smoke ceramic shards and also arrangements of pebbles, shells and seeds. But do not attempt the technique with fabrics as it will in all likelihood result in mess.

Spider's web

This is the building up of patterns of straight-sided geometric forms with

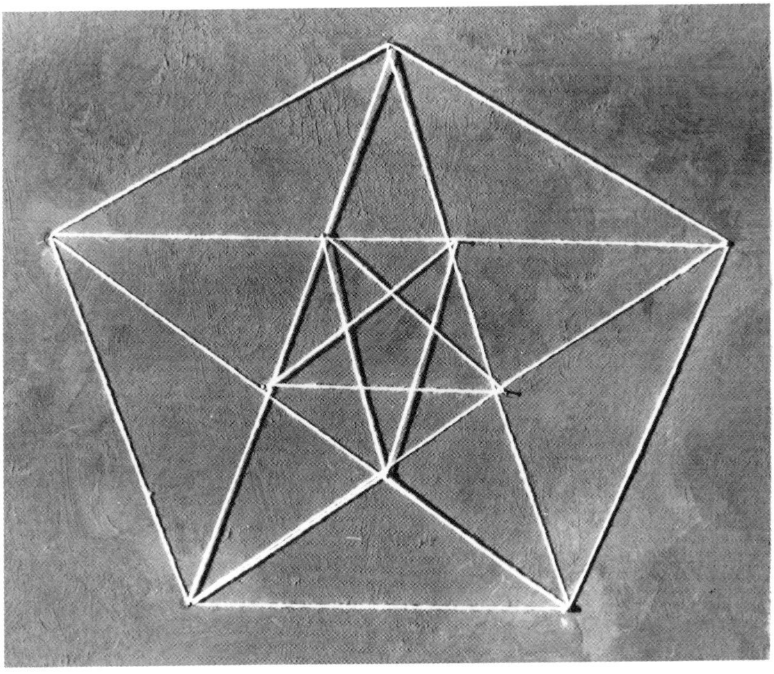

Spider's web

cottons, threads, wools and string passed between points marked by small pins. The webs may be either lying flat against the support or can be woven about 12 mm (½ in) up from the support.

Sponge dabbing

This is a way to quickly produce a speckled area of colour. Plastic sponges can be bought with quite a variety of texture, some with large holes, some with very small. If one of these is dipped into a fairly strong colour and then nearly rung out and it is dabbed on papers or cards interesting moss patterns will be made.

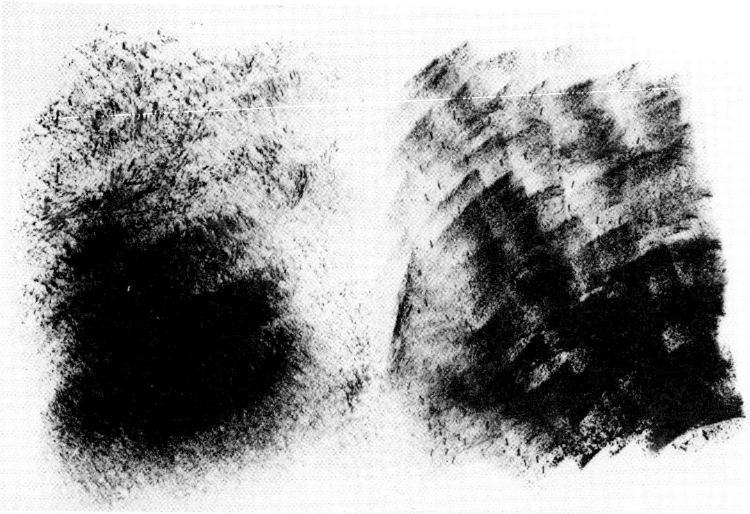

Dabbing with plastic sponge on the left, and with a square piece of foam on the right

Spatter and spray

These methods can be used to cover areas of paper, card and most textiles with a broken and graduated spotted appearance that can to a degree be controlled. Leaves, cut-out card shapes, keys, washers, fishbones and such like can be laid on to a support and then be given a spatter with colour. When the objects are lifted off their ghost image will remain.

Spatter is the simplest to do. Just dip a stiff bristled brush in the colour and then, holding it over the area to be treated, run a finger through the bristles. Spray can be done with a professional airbrush or one of those right-angled atomisers intended for blowing fixative on to a charcoal or pastel drawing. The method may also be worked with the aerosols containing colour. Whichever way is tried, it is a good plan to put in a little practice on scraps of newspaper first because the technique can be difficult to control.

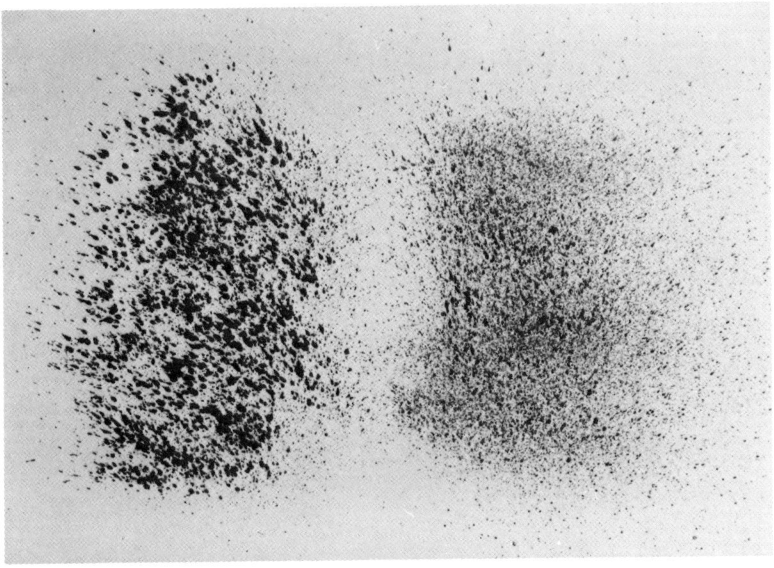

Spatter from a hog brush on the left, and from a fine nylon brush on the right

Texture with paints and plasters

Experiments with raising marks on paint and plaster will show that there are a number of ways of introducing some special effect in areas of a composition.

Oil paints can be given various treatments with brushes and knives which can produce quite rugged textures, the snag being that the colours take so long to dry. Most oil colours can take up to seven days to get skin-dry and if the paint is really thick it can take several years to harden right through. Texturing can be undertaken with powder colours mixed with pastes and size, but the results are liable to crack and flake off. Powder colours can be mixed with acrylic medium and satisfactory results obtained, but the best course is to use the acrylic paints themselves. The stiffness can be increased if desired by mixing some marble dust, kaolin or whiting into the colours. Acrylic paints will normally skin-dry in about two hours and harden through overnight even when the colours have been put on with a thickness up to about 12 mm ($\frac{1}{2}$ in). As with oils the acrylics can be manipulated with brushes and painting knives and may also be shaped with combs, scrapers and other suitable tools.

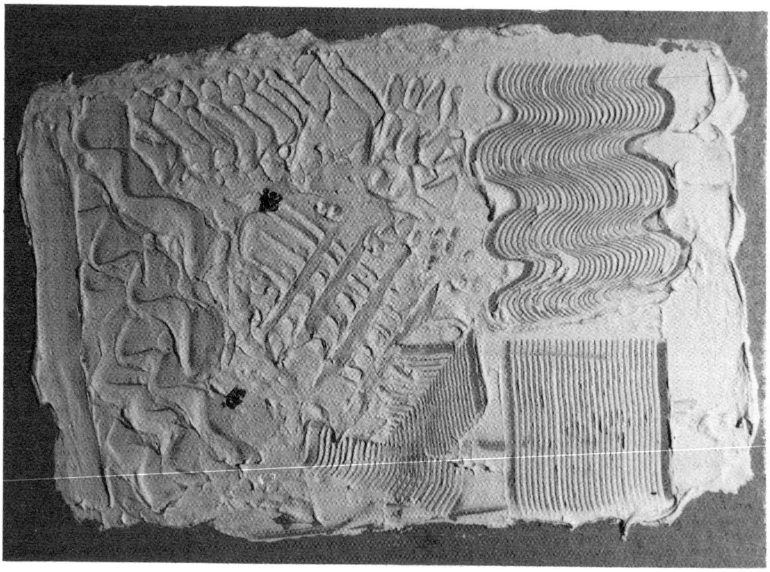

Texture into moist plaster

Plaster of Paris, other proprietary quick-setting plasters and gesso can all be treated as above to bring up an interesting surface. They may also be deep engraved, chiselled, scraped and sanded to the surface desired. If a rugged plaster surface is to be painted after treatment, it should be first isolated, either with size or shellac, to prevent the colours sinking in and thus losing their brilliance and strength.

Tissue overlays

This is the laying of different colour tissue papers over one another to achieve varying colour mixes. Yellow over blue for a green, blue over yellow for a different green, likewise with other colours. Two, three or more coloured tissues may be overlaid to produce many degrees of subtle tint and tone change.

The coloured tissues are best laid on a good white stout card. A suitable adhesive can be prepared from one part acrylic medium to one part of water, or the medium can be used neat. With a broad brush, lay the adhesive on the card and smooth the first tissue into it; brush on more acrylic and lay the second coloured tissue, brush over more acrylic and either leave to dry or put down a third tissue and continue the process. The smoking technique mentioned earlier can be very effective with this tissue work.

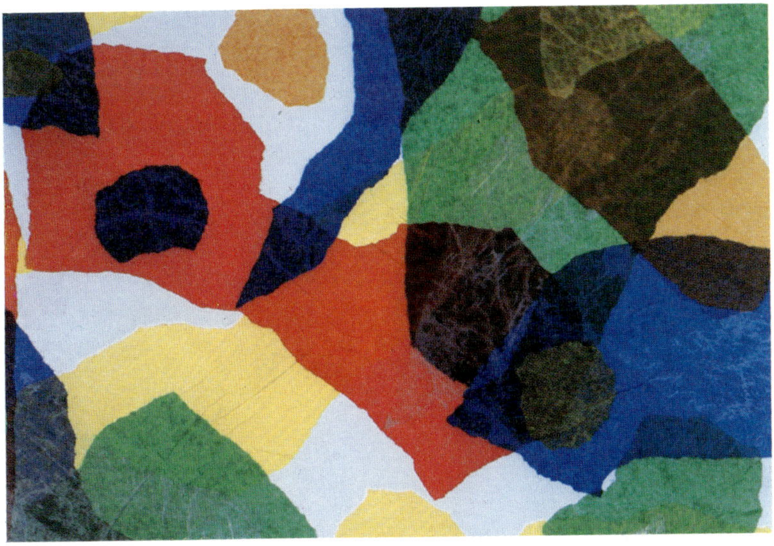

Overlaid coloured tissues

Titre poème

This consists of arrangements of patches of cut-out writing, lettering or printing pasted down to form an image, either abstract or realist. It was a form of collage practised by the Dadaists and the Surrealists in the early part of this century. Although water pastes will suffice, it is better to use a diluted acrylic medium as this will not only hold the patches better but also help to preserve them from fading and yellowing.

Torn paper

This is the use of torn as opposed to scissor-cut papers. Ordinary newspaper is quite suitable and often lively designs can be built up either with the pieces completely stuck down or better still only partially, simulating for example a bird's feathers or some layered texture. Pastes, natural glues, contacts, acrylic medium and PVA can all be used.

Transfer and stencil letters and figures

Passages can be worked with these rather in the manner of a *titre poème*. The letters that are taken off the transfer sheets by rubbing from the front with a burnisher will adhere quite well on most paper, card and wood surfaces if they are smooth. Their adhesion can be strengthened by brushing over with PVA or acrylic medium.

Stencils can be bought in a wide selection of letter and figure types, or they may be cut from thin card or imitation parchment. They can be 'printed' on to the support or other materials including most textiles either by dabbing the colour on with a piece of cotton wool or with a short bristled brush.

Veining

A somewhat elusive technique which is worked with coloured tissue papers. The procedure is first of all to brush a mixture of one part acrylic medium and three parts water over a support. This may be a smooth white card,

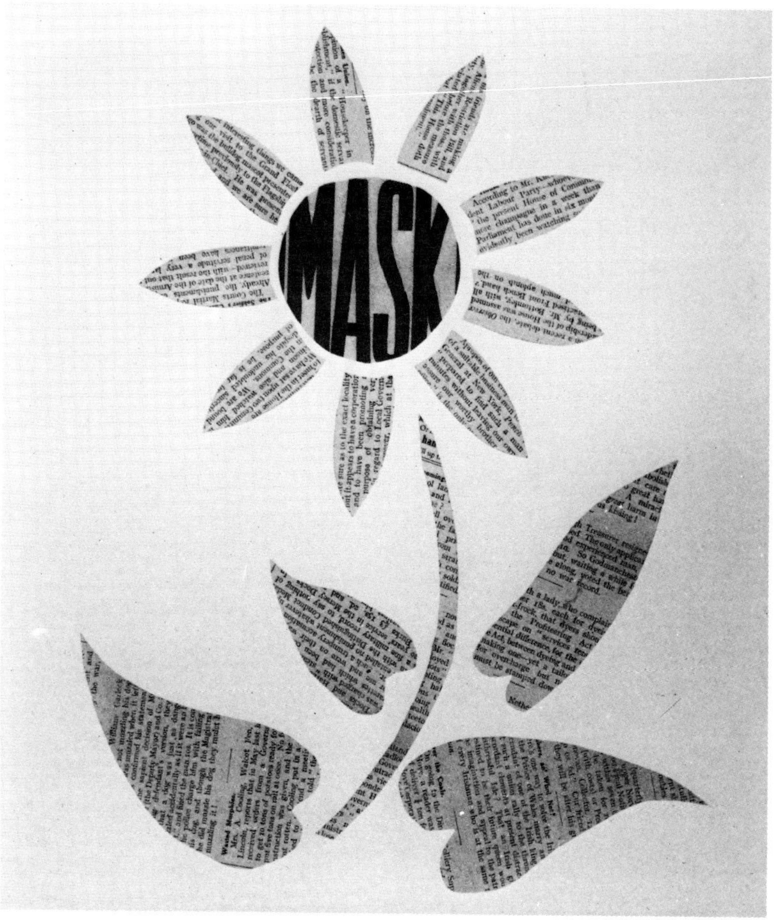

Titre poème

heavy smooth white paper or a sheet of glass. While the acrylic is still very fluid, place a sheet of tissue straight down into it. Almost at once the moistening tissue starts to buckle and crease, conditions which with other methods you would try to remove by lifting and smoothing. But not this time; try to manipulate the forming creases by working at them with a brush dipped into more acrylic mixture. To a degree they can be encouraged to form systems of veining and what looks like cracking which will show up dark as it will be formed from about three thicknesses of the tissue. A second method which can produce a more complex veining is to first crumple the sheet of tissue into a tight ball. Open it out flat again and then proceed as above.

Wax resist

Broken, speckled and haphazard colour effects may be desirable with some subjects. Passages may need simulated pieces of old stonework, flaking plaster, coarse bark impressions or just broken areas of paint made up of scattered droplets. It is simplest to prepare these on separate sheets of paper that can dry out and then be cut to size.

First rub the surface of the paper with an ordinary candle—beeswax is really too tacky—being sure that there is an adequate covering. Holding the sheet at an angle to the light will soon show if any areas have been missed.

After the waxing is completed the colour can be brushed over it. The paint chosen must be watercolour as oil or acrylic will not work. The consistency is important because if it is too thick it will not resist and if too thin the effect will not come through. A little practice on scraps of paper will soon determine the right dilution. The broken effects achieved by using wax and watercolour in this way can be continued over previously-laid wax and colours as many times as desired.

Protection

It was suggested earlier that fragile materials could be treated with a fine spray of diluted acrylic medium, and to this could be added another spray treatment. Owing to the nature of some of the materials that may have been used, there are two pests that may attack your collage. Edibles in the way of textiles and vegetable matter can attract insects. These may be woodworm, clothes moth or firebrat; the last mentioned delighting in over-dry pastes and natural glues with paper. A light application of a proprietary protective liquid should discourage these. The second enemy can be various unsightly mould growths. These will manifest themselves in damp conditions; papers, natural glues and vegetable matter are all prone to attack, the more so if the picture is hanging in a corner where there could

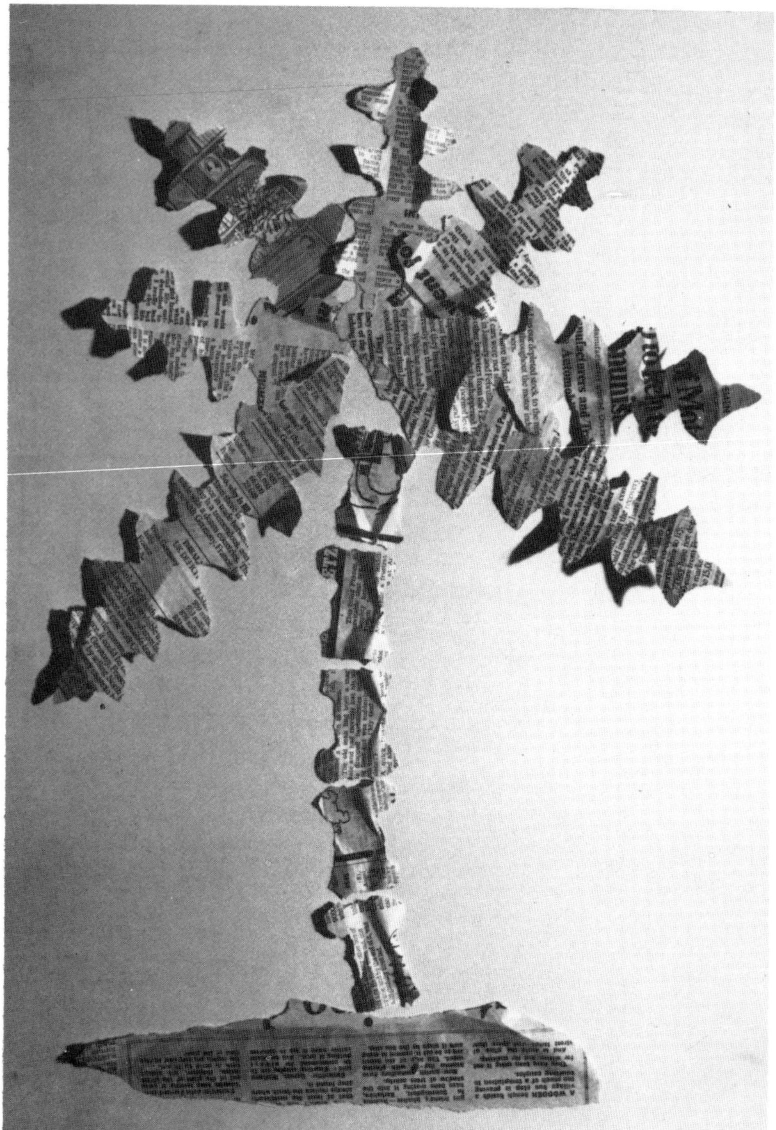

Torn paper

be a pocket of stagnant air. Again a light spray can give protection, this time of thymol dissolved to saturation point in alcohol.

Framing

The framing of a collage is really a matter of personal taste. But in general where there is a lot of movement in the design and there have been many different materials used a simple channel or rod frame may answer best. If the relief is fairly deep, a protective measure can be to have the frame of nothing more than narrow planks about 25 mm (1 in) thick and perhaps about 25 mm (1 in) deeper than the highest relief areas.